FEAST OF THE MORRIGHAN

A GRIMOIRE FOR THE DARK LADY OF THE EMERALD ISLE

by Christopher Penczak

COPPER CAULDRON
PUBLISHING

CREDITS

Writing: Christopher Penczak

Editing: Steve Kenson

Cover Design: Derek Yesman

Interior Art: Christopher Penczak, Derek O'Sullivan

Interior Design & Publishing: Steve Kenson

Proofreading: Karen and Shirli Ainsworth, Rebecca Chavez, Shae Morgan, Sharon Morrison

For more information visit:

www.christopherpenczak.com

www.coppercauldronpublishing.com

ISBN 978-0-9827743-6-6

Printed in the U.S.A.

"Morrigan, The Phantom Queen" by Derek O'Sullivan

ACKNOWLEDGEMENTS

To the Great Queen Herself for the inspiration and mission of my life. Thank you for rescuing me when I didn't know I needed to change.

A very special thanks to David Rankine and Sorita d'Este, authors of *The Guises of the Morrigan: Irish Goddess of Sex and Battle: Her Myths, Powers and Mysteries*. Their work provided a valuable guide to the old texts and myths, as well as fresh scholarly perspectives on the Great Goddess. Their inspiration deepened my relationship with the Goddess and her lore. I am very grateful. Thank you.

To Rosina Mostardini, soul sister to me and founder of *The Heart of the Morrighan Community Interfaith Temple*. Thank you for all your love and support and blessings.

To Kala Trobe, soul sister and giver of wise counsel, for my first visit to Avalon, and for arranging my fateful meeting with the Crow upon the Tor. Thank you! Words cannot say…

To Patricia Monaghan for your expertise on Ireland, all around good advice and true friendship even when our paths wander far and wide. Much love and blessing to you.

To Sharynne Mcleod NicMhacha, for being an excellent teacher in traditional Celtic practices, and urging me to work directly with source material.

To Laurie Cabot for first introducing me to the Celtic gods, and in particular to Macha, and for the phrase "Feast of the Morrigan."

To all of the Temple of Witchcraft for supporting my work in the world that She started and letting it become "our" Great Work.

To my family Steve Kenson, Adam Sartwell, and Ronald Penczak. Thank you for your love and support.

To Rosalie, may Macha fly with you always.

OTHER BOOKS BY CHRISTOPHER PENCZAK

City Magick (Samuel Weiser, 2001)

Spirit Allies (Samuel Weiser, 2002)

The Inner Temple of Witchcraft (Llewellyn, 2002)

The Inner Temple of Witchcraft CD Companion (Llewellyn, 2002)

Gay Witchcraft (Samuel Weiser, 2003)

The Outer Temple of Witchcraft (Llewellyn, 2004)

The Outer Temple of Witchcraft CD Companion (Llewellyn, 2004)

The Witch's Shield (Llewellyn, 2004)

Magick of Reiki (Llewellyn, 2004)

Sons of the Goddess (Llewellyn, 2005)

The Temple of Shamanic Witchcraft (Llewellyn, 2005)

The Temple of Shamanic Witchcraft CD Companion (Llewellyn, 2005)

Instant Magick (Llewellyn, 2005)

The Mystic Foundation (Llewellyn, 2006)

Ascension Magick (Llewellyn, 2007)

The Temple of High Witchcraft (Llewellyn, 2007)

The Temple of High Witchcraft CD Companion (Llewellyn, 2007)

The Living Temple of Witchcraft Vol. I (Llewellyn, 2008)

The Living Temple of Witchcraft Vol. I CD Companion (Llewellyn, 2008)

The Living Temple of Witchcraft Vol. II (Llewellyn, 2009)

The Living Temple of Witchcraft Vol. II CD Companion (Llewellyn, 2009)

The Witch's Coin (Llewellyn, 2009)

The Three Rays of Witchcraft (Copper Cauldron Publishing, 2010)

The Plant Spirit Familiar (Copper Cauldron Publishing, 2011)

The Witch's Heart (Llewellyn, 2011)

The Gates of Witchcraft (Copper Cauldron Publishing, 2012)

Buddha, Christ, Merlin: Three Wise Men for Our Age (Copper Cauldron Publishing, 2012)

Table of Contents

TABLE OF FIGURES

FOREWORD

Decades ago, my early Wiccan mentors conducted me and my fellow students through guided meditations, expecting us all to get visions of love and light. I was the sole student in that class who didn't get such visions. When I told them of my vision of the queen of shadows in her raven cloak showing up before me, they looked alarmed and told me I was doing something wrong. Looking back, decades later, I plainly see that their guided meditation was entirely successful and that my perception was crystal clear that evening, even though my results were incomprehensible to my mentors. The aspect of the divine that came to me in those meditations was the Morrighan. She's been with me ever since. My relationship with her is one of the reasons that part of my Craft name is Cuhulain, since Cu Cucuhainn was one of her protégés.

Being a martial artist who is ex-military, and having pursued a thirty six year career in law enforcement, the Morrighan is the principle female deity that I work with. My relationship with her mirrors Christopher's: I have found her to have the capacity to be very loving and caring, but not necessarily gentle. Her lessons and solutions are direct and sometimes harsh. Devote yourself to her, and she is certain to aid you, but equally certain to challenge you.

Christopher notes that not much survives in myth describing the Morrighan or her three aspects, and points out that she often is described in a "supporting role" for other Celtic deities and heroes. I believe that the reason for this is that she is a difficult aspect of the divine to define, elusive and mysterious. I think that Christopher would agree with me when I suggest that being a warrior Goddess, the Morrighan keeps a low profile, hence the meaning of her name: "Phantom Queen". She's fluid, a shapeshifter, and that's a necessary quality for any effective warrior. That's always been the way she is with me. From time to time, she has appeared to me in all her glory, but most often you only sense that she is there, a shadow in your peripheral vision. Her lesson or message is crystal clear, but you won't necessarily see the teacher.

Christopher speaks of "the notion of how the warrior serves the Goddess, serves the land, and lives in right accord. Those that do not are destined to failure." As the head of the Order of Scáthach, a Pagan order of Knights that promotes living according to a code of chivalry and right action, I agree. This is a lesson that not just modern day warriors, but everyday people need to learn. Being a warrior isn't about fighting, it is about being effective. It isn't about using your hands, it is about using your head. It is about right action and taking charge of your life, and this is a lesson that the Morrighan will indeed teach you. She will dare you, inspire you, provoke you, test you, make you see your power, and compel you to use it to be all you can be. The Morrighan is a Goddess to inspire you to great achievements. She requires you to banish weakness, which means you must face your fears and leave comfort behind. She won't fight your battles: She'll show you how to fight them yourself. This is why she stays in the shadows. It is you that she is pushing into the limelight, you that she wants to be seen. She wants to you to be glorious.

In this book Christopher gives you meditations to explore a relationship with this misunderstood aspect of the divine. Do you dare to work with the Morrighan in any or all of her aspects? Then this book is for you.

— Kerr Cuhulain, Preceptor General, Order of Scáthach

INTRODUCTION

It is said that the Celtic Gods, beyond all other pantheons, choose their own. Call to the Greek and Roman pantheons, or call to Isis or Thor, and you will usually receive a response to your prayer. While the Celtic gods will hear and sometimes even answer for a time, they will choose you as their own only if they recognize you. You can't always choose them. You need to be called. And from the past experiences that have led me here, I have to agree.

I didn't choose to work with the Morrighan. She chose to work with me and made her presence known, first through her manifestation as Macha. The Craft tradition I first studied was a modern Celtic one, blending Hermetic and Egyptian ideas with the myths of Ireland and Wales. We called upon totems for the four directions, and later Celtic deities associated with those totems. To the south was the element of Air, and the Crow, and the crow goddess Macha. While also associated with Horses and Faeries, we focused on her crow aspects for ritual. I cannot consider myself talented in my first experiences of magick. When someone described the energy of ritual, I must admit for a long time, I did not feel anything. No presence. No tingle. No goose-bumps. Sometimes an intuition, and my magick worked more often than not. My spellcraft was good. But when we called to the South, I felt a breeze, even indoors. Particularly indoors, which is what got my attention. Then I saw a shadow. That shadow became a figure. Then the figure began to talk to me, whispering to me. And that is how I was introduced to the goddess Macha. No longer could I place my ritual evocations in the realm of pure psychology. Something very real was happening, outside the scope of my imagination, unintentionally and unbidden, but there nonetheless. My craft utterly changed when Macha came into my life.

My experiences in circle then led to my meditation. Performing acts of simple core shamanism, my visions were filled with the Tree of the World, the cosmic axis filled with crows. Horses would circle the tree. And when I ventured forth in vision to the spirit world, there she would be, waiting for me. Black feathered cloak. Regal. Intimidating. And, despite many people's historic perceptions of her, patient and loving. She became my matron deity, marking me as her priest, to do her work in the world, though initially, much of our work seemed to be about my own healing and education.

Through her presence and tutelage, my Craft advanced by leaps and bounds. I was better at ritual, spirit contact and herb craft, though the psychic experiences slowed down. It seemed rather than being barraged by a lot of extraneous information, I was given only the information I needed, both in day to day life, and in my practice doing psychic readings and tarot counseling for others. My focus became honed.

All of this prepared me for her next step. I never envisioned myself as a metaphysical teacher, at least not professionally. My degree is in music performance, and I had aspirations to be a rock star, and then later a more serious singer songwriter. After college and my initial Craft training when my relationship with Macha began, and through the tutoring of a daughter of Macha who was scholarly and a reconstructionist Celtic shamanic practitioner, I deepened my relationship further. I began work in the Boston music scene working for a small record label with national distribution. After less than three years working there, where I was leading a monthly meditation group back in New Hampshire, I had more intense visions of Macha. She was face to face with me and would only say, "You need to teach more." I would give excuses why I couldn't or didn't want to, and I would suddenly be snapped back from my meditation into a waking state. Every time I tried to meditate, the same thing happened: A request to teach more, an excuse why I couldn't and the sudden shock of being snapped back to the waking world. This continued for weeks. Finally, I agreed to teach more. Three days later, I was laid off from my job.

I couldn't get a new job answering phones, and after many strange and unsuccessful temporary job assignments in offices that ended with the last place burning down the day before I started, I gave up the search for traditional and steady employment. My only guidance in meditation was Macha's face again saying, "Now you can teach more." She also told me that if I did this, I would never really have to worry about money again. I would be taken care of by her and the gods. I would be doing my Will, and theirs. I began writing a book about my urban magickal experiences and put up flyers for a basic meditation class and soon had a full house of new students and a publishing contract.

My first class developed from the monthly Moon gathering into more esoteric workshops on Witchcraft, magick and past lives, also with far more success than I would have anticipated. The class expanded into a system. The system grew into a tradition. The tradition created a legal religious body recognized by the federal government, the Temple of Witchcraft, where training continues in a variety of forms. Though the life of a writer and teacher is not always stable, she was right; I've never had a month that I could not meet my financial obligations and with planning and strategy, have never really gone without any necessities or even basic comforts that I've desired.

While at times I feel like I've veered away from Macha, exploring my relationship with the Weaver Goddess, the Ancestors, the Fey, alchemy, Lugh, Hecate and Ceridwen, my path always seems to lead me back to her, and from her, deeper into the mysteries of the Morrighan. While traveling on a book tour, I met an amazing woman, a soul sister touched by the Morrighan's heart, and we instantly recognized the bond of family. We were able to verify mystical experiences and share our love of the Goddess as kin. My understanding of Hermeticism and Polytheism grew through my relationship with Ceridwen, and then the Arthurian Mysteries, looking for mythic and magickal, if not historic, links to the Morrighan. I understood the nature of the Dark Lady in her many forms, and found wisdom of the Morrighan in other cultures and times. Unlike other goddesses, there is not much surviving involving her myths specifically, as she often plays a support role in the myths of others. Information on her ancient cults of worship, offerings and symbols were never recorded, so we are left only to speculate, look for parallel information in other cultures, and of course, ask her ourselves.

She has always been with me, sometimes silently at my side while I am experiencing the mysteries of the east through yoga and Reiki, or more directly, in my magick and shamanic healing. Those who have the eyes to see always note a very tall, dark woman in a black cloak, almost like wings. Some mistake her for Isis, or her sister Nephthys. Others see Freya or even another three in one, Hecate, but those who have been touched by her heart know the Morrighan when they see and feel her. They see her in the hearts and minds of their sisters and brothers, all touched by her presence. I am comforted to know she is with me in all that I do. She lives within my heart, and I, within hers.

This book is a work of devotion to her. Guided by her heart and mind, to my own. It started with a poetic song, the first of this book, that haunted my mind no matter what I did. Once I committed it to type, the rest of the book started flowing. I called it *The Feast of the Morrighan* in the sense of the ritual feast as being an offering. This work is an offering to her as much as any other I have given. Today there are many books on goddesses such as Hecate, Lilith, Ma'at and Isis, but there is very little on this popular goddess. There are only a few books gathering together her lore. The work is also a feast for her devotees, something to nourish us in the development of our relationship with her. It is something to share. *The Feast of the Morrighan* is part research of classic texts, part personal experience and partly my own understanding as a priest of Macha. It is not the only view of this goddess, but meant to inspire your own direct relationship. Many would take issue with my wide net of cultural exploration in trying to understand her, as well as my decidedly Hermetic views on divinity in general. There are as many questions to ponder as there are answers given here, perhaps more. The poetry is my own unless otherwise noted, though inspired greatly by the works of the past. At times it was a battle to write, not flowing freely from my fingers, but I wouldn't expect anything easy from such a goddess. The rituals are in the context of modern Witchcraft, and not necessarily a strict Celtic Reconstructionist Paganism. They are drawn directly from my own practice. May it guide you in your own journey with these dark ladies.

CHAPTER ONE
The Great Goddess

Who is the Morrighan? And even more importantly, *what* is the Morrighan? There is no easy answer. She is a mystery, and must be experienced to be understood, yet once experienced, words can fail to describe her.

Today we think of the Morrighan as a Celtic goddess, yet in all the Celtic literature that survives today, she is never explicitly stated as one. Like many of the Celtic deities, outright divinity is not proclaimed like it is with the Greek or Hindu gods. Their myths are recorded in a Christian, not Pagan era, leaving them in an ambiguous zone where the edges blur and the lines cease to have meaning. I think that perhaps this is where the Celtic gods like to be anyway. They are liminal creatures, and unlike the Greco-Roman gods, cannot be pinned down in explicit stories and a single realm of dominion. They are like us: multifaceted, complex, guided by seemingly human impulses and the inspiration of the divine, of the otherworld, where motives are not clearly known. The most powerful and wise have many areas of expertise, for knowledge and skill were greatly valued in Celtic society. Their wisdom was holistic, rather than compartmentalized or reductionist.

The Morrighan is so mysterious because she doesn't have one set identity. She is linked with a variety of other goddesses. They are similar, yet separate. Their relationship is often described as sisters, but it's difficult to tell who exactly her sisters are, as some names seem to simply be titles for her, or other goddesses.

Through these relationships, she embodies the great paradox, the great mystery of divinity. She is many and she is one. She is both of these things simultaneously. That is the paradox of the mysteries, of the ancient schools and traditions. Or at least this is one of the many paradoxes that the initiate experiences. It is in the paradox that the gateway to the mysteries, to a new consciousness beyond the limited, ordinary consciousness of everyday opens to us. For many Celtic-inspired practitioners, the Morrighan is the gateway into the mysteries of initiation.

Most Witches and Pagans are considered polytheistic, meaning they believe in many gods and goddesses. One only has to look at the mythology of almost any ancient or tribal people and see our gods are many. Yet the same cultures often believe in the unity of spirit, of a current of life, a web or circle, that runs through all things. We find this still existing today in tribal cultures. The later Hermeticists identified it with the Divine Mind, the One, the All, and we are all manifestations within this One Mind, including the gods. How can we be many and yet be fundamentally one? That is the mystery, and the experience of this paradox leads to a magickal initiation.

The Morrighan teaches us the fundamental flow of birth, life, death and rebirth through her many guises. Today she is most popularly seen as a triple goddess.

THE THREE WHO ARE ONE

When I first learned about the Morrighan from my own teachers, she was called a triple goddess. The triple goddess had become a popular image in modern Witchcraft. Many triple goddesses can be found across world cultures, and we saw them each as an expression of the one Goddess. Maiden, mother and crone was the first vision of the triple goddess presented to me, and the three were later related to the various fates of Greek, Roman and the Northern Traditions embodying past, present and future, as well as the goddesses of the Heavens, Earth and Underworld, the three shamanic worlds.

Yet as I explored more traditional sources, the Celtic triple goddess didn't usually follow such a neat division. The three would appear as three mothers, or three sisters. This didn't invalidate our maiden-mother-crone experiences, but deepened the mystery of the Morrighan, as she was different.

I was taught the Morrighan was one of the primary Irish goddesses, a goddess of battle and death, of sex and fertility and of wisdom and prophecy. Those three complex areas of interest didn't easily fit her various forms. One of her triad was not explicitly and only a goddess of battle and death. Another was not the matron of fertility with the last sister ruling over prophecy. All of her three forms would manifest all of these those qualities on some level, along with her association with land and magick in general. She would teach those whom she chose, and she would test those whom she taught. She wasn't the most simple and easily understood image of the goddess, like our more familiar images of the goddess of love, or the goddess of the Moon, but in truth, even those seemingly simple images are far more complex than most of us realize.

The Morrighan or Morrigan is usually her collective name, though sometimes the sisters would be referred to as the Morrigu or plurals as the Morrighans or the Morrigana. For this text, I tend to use the spelling with the "h," Morrighan, to denote the vast collective goddess and without the "h" when quoting other sources. At times the Morrighan was one of the three sisters, instead of a collective name or title. The name Morrighan is translated to mean "Great Queen" or "Phantom Queen" as she is linked with the Goddess of the Land itself, the Queen of the Land, specifically Ireland and the Queen of the Otherworld, the world of phantasms, faery folk and the dead that dwelt beneath the visible land. To the ancient Celt, the two lands were not that far apart, divided by a hedge, river or other permeable boundary.

Two triads of goddesses were most prominent in Neopaganism to describe this goddess. The first was Anu, Badb and Macha, while the second was Badb, Macha and Nemain. We would try to see the maiden, mother and crone in these figures respectively, but other than the stories of Macha giving birth to twins, becoming the mother, the fit was not easy. One of the most clear, yet least popularly quoted in Neopaganism, triads from Irish myth lists the three sisters as Morrigan, Badb and Macha. Other goddesses that have found their way into association with the Great Queen include Danu, Fea, Folta/Fodla, Banaba and Anann.

Over time, she has even been associated with a whole host of Celtic goddesses beyond the Irish lore, including Rhiannon, Modron, Epona, Cailleach, the Valkyries and the Arthurian figure of Morgana Le Fey. She takes many guises over our mythic landscape.

Speak to me of She of the Three Crows
Raven Clawed and Horse Hoofed
Red Maned and Feather Cloaked

Speak to me of She of the Black
Framed Against Blue Skies
Death against life
With sex standing at the gateway between

Speak to me of She of Good Counsel
Of the Dreaded Prophecy
of the Teaching and Tutoring
To Heroes and Witches

She draws Fire from the Sky
She stirs the Cauldron on the Isle
She sings with her sisters
And straddles the edge of the river of life and death

She rules the Phantoms as Queen
And rides with the Faery Hosts
She feasts upon the dead
And loves mortals and gods alike

She carries the Spear of Victory
She washes with the women at the ford
She grants the land with a kiss
And brings death to those who do not listen

Speak to me of She who is the Dark Lady
Black and White, Red and Grey
Three who hold the mystery of all
Three who will show you the way.

THE MOTHER OF THE GODS

Our first mythic encounter with the Morrighan comes with the Tuatha de Dannan. This is a race of gods, with their name literally meaning the Children of Danu, the mother of the gods. They come to Ireland in "flying ships" from the West, or from the Four Corners of the World, and settle in this new land. They are the mythic creatures from lands beyond what was known, coming to usher in a new age of civilization.

Ireland is colonized by a series of invasions, of various races that in turn dominate the other. While it's a story of Ireland, mythically Ireland and its invasions are seen as a microcosm for the cycles of creation in the world. Ireland is really the world. In this cosmology, it is the omphalos, the navel of the world, the center of all things. What happens to Ireland happens to the world. What happens to the people of Ireland happens to the people of the world. Perhaps this is not how the folklorist of old looked at these stories, but it is certainly the mythopoetic lens occultists see them through.

Many cultures believe in several preceding successive "ages" of consciousness, dominated by a particular race that embodies that consciousness. Each gives way to a new age, and a new race to embody it. The idea dominates the teachings of the Theosophical movement, the foundation of the New Age teachings. The founders of Theosophy, such as Madame Helena Blavatsky, sought to find the common world wisdom and unite both eastern and western mystery teachings. She had a huge influence on the occult, ceremonial and New Age movements, and in turn influenced every facet of Neopaganism. Similar teachings on the great ages are found in many cultures, particularly with the Greeks and Hindus, who mark the cosmic ages not with invasions, but with metals, and European folk traditions, which mark them with the ages of animals and trees. We are said to be on the cusp of such a change now ourselves, and the changes in culture, religion, values and information reflect an "invasion" of a new consciousness.

The Morrighan seemingly lands with the Tuatha as they colonize the Island of Ériu, or Ireland, and helps them defeat the current race of inhabitants, the Fir Bolgs. The Fir Bolgs are a race of deities more chaotic and wild, and some have been described as even demonic, but they are more akin to the Titans and Cyclops of Greek myth, while the Tuatha are roughly like the next generation of gods, the Olympians, brighter, more ordered and more "human" in shape and consciousness. Yet as the story progresses, the Morrighan seems to be somewhat separate from the Tuatha tribe. She is with them, but later it is implied that she is also beyond them.

In the first battle with the Fir Bolgs, the Morrighan, with Badb and Macha, are sorceresses, working their magick to attack the Tuatha's enemies, and prevent them from moving from Tara, the central hill where they were encamped, later to become the center of rulership for Ireland. In the First Battle of Moytura, the three Witch goddesses rained down sorcery, fire and red blood upon their enemies, preventing the Fir Bolgs from moving from the area for three days and three nights.

Later the three goddesses are a quartet, joined by Danu, making one of her rare appearances in the stories of the Tuatha. Usually she is unseen and unheard in these stories, a goddess of the gods themselves, and is often believed today by modern Pagans to be the embodiment of the living waters (such as the Danube River), the planet itself (a Celtic equivalent of the Earth Mother Gaia) or the universe itself (the starry Goddess). The Morrighan's relationship with Danu and the Tuatha de Dannan is an interesting part of her ever-evolving mystery.

In the next great war of the Tuatha, they face the race of the Fomorians. Regularly equated with the Fir Bolgs, the Fomorians are actually a race of seafaring pirates who possibly inhabited Ireland with the Fir Bolgs prior to the Tuatha's arrival. After the First Battle of Moytura, the Tuatha King Nuada is forced to abdicate the throne, as he lost a hand in battle, and the Tuatha required their king to be physically perfect. He peacefully abdicates to Bres, a half Fomorian and half Tuatha prince. Through Bres, the Fomorians demand tribute and eventually the Tuatha, unhappy with their new king and his other people, revolt, leading to the Second Battle of Moytura against the Fomorians.

In this tale, the Morrighan appears somewhat separate from the Tuatha de Dannan. On one hand, she gives her advice freely and incites the war. On the other, she must be petitioned for her advice and aid. Her motives are mysterious.

The Morrighan starts the battle, if not with the first blow, with the first words. The goddess ignites the fires of conflict among the Tuatha. She speaks to Lugh, one of the key warriors of the Tuatha army. She says, "Undertake a battle of overthrowing" and "Awake." He is outfitted with magickal weapons from the three sons of Danu: Brian, Luchar and Lucharba, who are also considered to be three sons of the Morrighan. So the power of the Morrighan is the engine that starts this revolt. She gives this counsel freely.

Later in the war, the Tuatha send the great god Dagda out to scout and spy on the Fomorians. An interesting choice, as the Dagda is described as titanic, a giant, suggesting his origin is of an earlier age. Gigantic gods always imply an elder power. Giant gods don't seem to make the best spies, and sometimes he is portrayed somewhat like a buffoon or clown, but as a very powerful and skilled god, perhaps they were chancing that his skill was more necessary than stealth. Or perhaps they chose him because of his titanic elder power, and they were sending their emissary into the depths of the land to the goddess for counsel. It was a mystical mission instead of a military one. Rather than find the Fomorians, he first finds the Morrighan, as she washes clothes at the ford, her hair in nine red tresses. This motif appears again with the Morrighan, as she is said to wash the blood out of the clothes of slain warriors.

The Morrighan and the Dagda make love at the ford. Here we have a sense of proportion for the Morrighan. If she can make love to the Dagda, she must be able to take on titanic proportions as well. She is described as having one foot on each bank of the river. She too is an elder power. She gives him battle advice and a promise to kill the Fomorian leader Indech herself, taking his "heart's blood and testicles." With it, she would bless the Tuatha warriors with his blood. While she gives blessing, her blessing must be sought out. She must be wooed by the Dagda. Her support was not automatic, or there would have been no need to seek her out.

The Dagda continues his scouting mission, and interacts with the Fomorians, using the rules of hospitality. With hospitality invoked, they cannot harm each other. This notion of hospitality might seem strange to modern people thinking of war, but codes of honor and hospitality in the ancient Pagan world, even among such supernatural creatures, are very different than what we understand today. As the Dagda returns he encounters another woman, Boand, the daughter of the Fomorian king, but often interpreted as another form of the Morrighan. They too have sex, and she provides information to the Dagda as well. Many retellings of the story join both encounters into one, with only the Morrighan as his lover, and believe the interaction occurred on Samhain Eve. The tale becomes a part of Samhain rituals among modern Witches and Wiccans today. Samhain is the liminal time when the worlds of the living and the dead come close together and anything is possible. What better day to learn how to send your enemies to the land of the dead and receive the blessing of the war goddess than on Samhain? It is a time of great power.

After a fierce battle between the two armies and the death of the Fomorian one-eyed warrior Balor by Lugh, the Fomorians are pushed into the sea and the Tuatha are the undisputed rulers of Ireland. The Morrighan gives a victory prophecy, which strangely concludes with the prophecy of the end of the world. At the end of the war, Lugh is made king of Ireland.

Implied in the courting is that the Morrighan is beyond both the Tuatha and Fomorians. Though previously seen as one of the Tuatha, her loyalty comes, but is not automatic. She is not limited to one side, to one identity. Perhaps the two tribes, mythically opposed to each other, come from a similar root, a similar point of origin before they diverged. Perhaps that source is the Morrighan, or if not the Morrighan, the goddess Danu. In Greek myth the Olympians were born from the earlier generation of Titans and freely mated with them. The Titans in turn came from the more cosmic parents of Gaia and Ouranus, and Danu has been compared to Gaia.

The Tuatha were described as black birds descending upon Ireland when they arrived, implying a connection to the crow or raven. The most prominent sacred animal of the Morrighan is the crow. The Morrighan instigates the war between the two tribes, but why? Is it her bloodlust? Or is she an agent of some other form of cosmic balance, seeking to move forces in the direction she sees fit? There was an unfair tithe, an unjust tribute, and life and nature are about appropriate exchange. Perhaps such a tax was unbalancing creation, for we must remember these are gods, and their currency is beyond what we think of as simple coin. Their every action has cosmic significance.

The Morrighan's wars bring change. Without change, life becomes stagnant and nothing evolves. The next age cannot come about. Destruction, while feared, is as much a part of nature and creation as anything else. All things must wither and fall away. Some gradually wither, and some are swiftly destroyed. Perhaps that is why she ends the successful battle with a doom-filled prophecy of the end of the world. Was it the end of the Tuatha's world, their age before dwelling in the depths, or the end of our current world, the current age, or the end of all creation?

While never explicitly stated in the Irish texts, I was taught to see the great Goddess and God, from a Celtic point of view, as the deities of Danu and Dagda. They were the twin primordial forces that manifest, sustain and destroy our worlds. Though the Dagda was also considered to be the son of Danu, the theme of sacred incest and mother and son pairings is not uncommon between gods in mythologies the world over. Witchcraft traditions often include the worship of the Great Mother and the God as both child and lover.

Danu is unseen, for she is the manifestation of the entire cosmos. Dagda is the benevolent father who guides and shelters, who brings the change of the seasons with his magick harp and whose cauldron provides sustenance to all those who are worthy. They are compared to Gaia and Uranus in their most cosmic aspects. I imagine that this understanding was some priestess' personal gnosis that became part of the tradition, yet it now theologically works for a large body of Celtic-oriented Witches.

So in seeing the Dagda have such a relationship with the Morrighan before such a momentous battle, and for them to be on such equal terms, if not the Morrighan being superior, it's hard not to see the Morrighan as such a supreme deity. Her role is greater than simply the instigator of battle, yet that is one way her purpose manifests. She is the goddess of change and necessity.

Out of the watery chaos
Rose the Isle that would be emerald.
Out of the water chaos that was creation
Rose the Goddess of the Land
Out of the water chaos
Rose the Mother, the First Matter of Creation

From that time,
The Isle was claimed
By the waters of chaos many times
Floods came and went
Creation and Destruction brought renewal.

Five invasions came to the Land.
Five tribes of children to the Great Mother.
Five to shape the land,
Five to make their mark,
But perhaps more are to come.

Some say the first to settle on the land after the Great Flood was Cessair
Cessair and her warrior women and three men
Inhabited the Isle after a great flood.
Only Fintan survived, using magick to transform into a salmon.
And rose to tell the tale of the invasions of Ireland.

The first true wave came with the Partholons, led by Partholon.
They were the first to battle the Fomorian, the nightmare people
And drive them out to the northern sea.
The Great Goddess came forth among them,
As Macha, daughter of Partholon.
Their time on the land was short.
In a single generation, they were killed by plague.
Only Tuan, nephew of Partholon, survived to tell the tale.

The second true wave came with the Nemedians, led by Nemed.

They were the second to Battle the Fomorians, the sea banished people

And were attacked on their way to the Emerald Isle.

They were reduced to nine survivors.

Nine survivors made their way to Ériu.

Nine survivors rebuilt their people in a new land.

The Great Goddess came forth among them as well,

As Macha, wife of Nemed.

Macha, the prophet.

Macha the seer.

She foresaw the coming battles upon the land.

Her visions broke her heart

And twelve days later she was dead and returned to the land.

The Nemedians fought the Fomorians again.

Defeated, they were divided into three.

A third went to Greece to be enslaved and return as the Fir Bolgs.

A third went to North of England and became the Britons.

A third went to the four corners of the world to seek wisdom

And returned as the Tuatha de Dannan.

The third true wave came with the Fir Bolgs, led by Sláine Mac Dela

The Fir Bolgs, returning from slavery from the lands to the East.

They were the first to establish the Sacred Kingship upon the Emerald Isle.

They were the first to rule from the Hill of Tara

They were the first to make war with the Tuatha de Dannan

In the First Battle of Moytura

The last king of the Fir Bolgs, Eochaidh Mac Eirc, husband of Tailitiu,

Killed by the Morrighan.

The fourth true wave came with the Tuatha de Dannan, led by Nuada.

The Children of Danu descended upon the land like black birds in flight.

They brought with them the four sacred hallows from the four sacred cities.

With them came the Spear, the Sword, the Cauldron Cup and the Sacred Stone.

With them came magick.

The Children of Danu battled the Fir Bolgs, the First Kings
They battled the Fomorians, the nightmare people of the sea
And they won.
With them was the Morrighan, triple sisters, wise in magick.
They ruled 'til the coming of humanity, and they rule in secret still.
They rule from the mirror world beneath the hills where magick still lives in plentitude.

The fifth true wave came with the Milasians, led by the magick of Amergin.
The sons of Mil meet the mothers of daughters of the land,
Ériu, Banba and Fódla.
The sons of Mil defeat the Kings and husbands of the land,
Mac Cuill, Mac Cecht, and Mac Gréine.
And the three sons of Mil from eight survive and are named kings of Ireland,
Eber, Eremon, and Amergin.
The time of humanity rose
As the world awaits the sixth invasion.

THE MOTHER OF THE MORRIGHAN

In the subsequent invasions, the reigning Tuatha are in turn invaded by the Milesians. Those would become the modern human Irish. Rather than fight a noble people with magick of their own, exemplified in the Druid Amergin, the Tuatha de Danann realized their time was done, their age complete and rather than fight, withdrew into the land. Or at least that is the story the Irish tell us, as the direct descendents of the Milesians.

There the Tuatha created a mirror world, an otherworld or underworld where they dwelled in perfect peace and harmony with the spirits, and left the physical world above for the humans. They maintained relationships with many humans. In particular, the Morrighan has a powerful relationship with the semi-human hero Cu Chulainn. The Tuatha became the gods and spirits to the Milesians, and with the rise of Christianity were seen more as the Faeries of the land. The Morrighan was seen as a queen of spirits, phantoms and faeries. Is she the Queen of the Tuatha de Dannan? She's never explicitly named thus, but in some ways, her title as Great Queen and their desire for her blessing in the Second Battle of Moytura might be evidence of such.

The Milesians were met by three goddesses: Ériu (Érie), Banba and Fódla. These three sisters are considered the goddesses of sovereignty, the manifestation of the land itself, and the Milesians promised that Ériu's name would come first in reference to the land, though Banba and Fódla are still poetic references to Ireland. The English name Ireland comes directly from Ériu.

The mother of the three goddesses was named Ernmas, who was also seen as an embodiment of the land. Ernmas was described specifically as a Witch as well, with her name meaning "iron death." Did that refer to death by sharpened weapon, or death by the magickal power of iron? Considered one of the Tuatha, as her father was Nuada of the Silver Hand, the first king of the Tuatha and their leader when they came to Ireland, she gave birth to a variety of deities, particularly in trinities. Beyond Ériu and her sisters, she gave birth to the "war" goddesses Badb, Macha, and Morrigan. Geoffrey Keating, known in Irish as Seathrun Ceitinn, was a 17th Century Roman Catholic priest best known for his work *The History of Ireland*. He equated the three land goddesses with the three wars. Ériu was described as a beautiful woman who could take the form of a white-gray crow, just as the Morrighan sisters could take the form of black crows. Each of the sovereignty sisters was a different aspect of the war sisters. Ériu in particular was related to Badb. So if in turn Badb is an aspect of the Morrighan, then the Morrighan is an embodiment of the land itself and bestower of sovereignty.

Paradoxically, Danu was also considered to be a daughter of Ernmas and Delbaeth, putting her in the same generation as Morrigan, Macha, and Badb. How would that be possible, as Nuada, grandfather of Ernmas, was one of the Children of Danu, unless there were two figures named Danu? Like the webs of Egyptian mythology, with its Horus the Elder and Horus the Younger figures often confused, is there a Danu the Elder and Danu the Younger at play here? Also paradoxically, Macha, in this earliest incarnation, was the wife of Nuada, the first king of the Tuatha. Did Macha marry her grandfather in another story of sacred incest? Or is there more than one Macha in this tale? The genealogy of gods is not quite as clear cut as one might hope, adding to the mystery. It seems that all these Goddesses lead us back to the origin of the gods themselves.

Evocation of Ernmas

Mother of the Great Mother,
Mother of the Great Queen.
Power before the Timeless Power,
When the world was new.

Ernmas,
Iron Death.
Ernmas,
Primal Land.
Ernmas,
Pangaea of the Emerald Isle.

Land Mother
Grand Mother
Mother of Ériu
Mother of Banba
Mother of Fódla

Witch Mother
War Mother
Mother of Badb
Mother of Macha
Mother of Morrigan

Ernmas,
Iron Death.
We call to you.

THE MOTHER OF ALL

The Morrighan, in her various aspects, keeps leading us back beyond the typical image of the war goddess, and emphasizes a connection to the land, and to the Great Mother. How can so many goddesses be the Queen of the Land and bestower of its sovereignty? Perhaps they are all one, a central source with many facets. Children of one deity are often the manifestation of that same deity to another generation, to another world. They can be embodiments, similar to the Hindu concept of avatars, in a new world. Does the power of Danu manifest in her children?

One of the Morrighan's triple deities, Anu or Annan, is seen as another name for Danu, mother of the Tuatha de Dannan, and in fact in one Fir Bolg battle, she is present with the sorcerous sisters. The author of *The Book of Leinster* equates the Morrighan directly with Danu, in reference to the hills, the Paps of Anu, or Breast of the goddess Anu/Danu. Danu was possibly considered her proper name. Is the Morrighan more than one goddess in the tribe of gods, but a manifestation of Danu? Is Danu the Great Mother of All, and not just the race of the Gods?

Danu has been equated with the Welsh mother goddess Don, as well as the Welsh Modron and Gaulish Matronna. Much like Danu, Don is considered the mother of the Welsh gods, yet is just as enigmatic as Danu, not appearing to take direct action in any of the conflicts of her children, and for the most part, nowhere in sight. Is this because she is everywhere and nowhere at all, being the mother of all and the manifestation of all?

While soft polytheism is unpopular today in reconstructionist circles, this a view of the goddess, at least in regard to the guises of the Morrighan. Most seeking to explore specific cultures more deeply look at ancient Pagans, such as the Celts, as hard polytheists, seeing each deity as separate and distinct, individual entities. They look at soft polytheism, a tendency to see the unity and oneness of a variety of deities and to see cultural similarities as links between deities, as an unwanted influence in Neopaganism from Hermeticism, Judeo-Christianity and modern psychology. Yet we don't really know what the mystics of the ancient Pagan cultures, particularly the Celts, really believed or experienced in their mysteries.

We know the philosophers and sages of Pagan Greece and Rome often equated their own gods with the gods of foreigners, particularly Egyptians and the Celts. Julius Caesar proclaimed that the Celts worshiped Mercury, not because they believed in the Mercury of the Romans or the Hermes of the Greeks, but the attributes of one of their main gods resembled Mercury the most, in Caesar's estimation. This view of similarities not only in cultural mythology but in the human experience is usually the dominant view of the initiate into the Western mysteries, Witchcraft included.

All of these various incarnations of the gods give a picture of Celtic polytheism more akin to the Hindus, which both share a common Indo-European source. In Hinduism, there are various manifestations of the same gods, in cosmic, terrestrial and localized forms. None invalidate the other, but add to the mystery of divine nature and the richness of experience. The paradox is part of the religious mystery.

When we look at the mercurial guises of these goddesses of war, sovereignty, land and motherhood, we see the mystery teaching of the ages, as framed by occultist Dion Fortune. "All gods are one God and all goddesses are one Goddess, and there is one initiator." That is what my own experience has been with this great lady. She manifests as she needs, from the personal ally and stern teacher to the celestial mother of all things, trifold and beyond human comprehension, rotating with her sisters in directions that cannot be seen or understood. From those cosmic experiences, I've had kinship with other manifestations of the one Goddess, yet have not lost my personal connection and tutelary relationship with Macha and the greater Morrighan.

In this sense, the Morrighan is the one initiator. She isn't a facet of one unknowable god, an unreal projection, but a paradox and mystery. All her guises are as separate and individual as all of us humans, plants and animals, yet all of us individuals are united by one life force within us, and one creation surrounding us in which we have our life and being. That is just part of the great mystery. You must answer our initial questions, who and what is the Morrighan? She is a mystery, and only by entering the mystery will we find our answers.

Invocation to the Morrighan as Universal Mother

Mother of the Emerald Isle
Mother of all life
Anu, Danu, Morrighan
Mother of Beauty and Strife

Daughters of Ernmas
Mother of the Time Before
Ériu, Banba and Fódla
Guardian and the Secret Door

Mother of the Black Crows
Children of the Ninth Wave
Don, Modron, Matronna
Fertile Womb and Deepest Grave

With the Rivers Flowing
Filled with Waters and Starry Light
Anu, Danu, Morrighan
We call you in this rite.

IMRAM TO THE GREAT MOTHER

Imram literature is a writing style found particularly in Irish poetry, though the concept can be found in other cultures and traditions under different names. *Imram* means "voyage" and a notable example is *The Voyage of Bran*. It is a story that depicts a journey of heroes and gods to fantastic lands. While it might contain historic elements, it usually exhibits an otherworldly nature. Some see it almost as an equivalent to the Egyptian and Tibetan books of the dead.

Today, many magickal practitioners believe that the imram literature is based upon shamanic journeys by past magickal practitioners, the Druids, Bards and Witches of the tradition. Their visions pass into oral, and then written, history. When listening to the Imram, one can almost experience the journey with the characters, much like today's guided visions, pathworkings and meditations.

Teachers of magickal journey and spirit flight, myself included, walk a fine line balancing the use of traditional imagery that has successfully been used before, and being open to the journeyer's own experiences and magickal point of view. Traditional imagery and correspondences not only focus the experience, but ground the practitioner in a tradition. The practitioner thereby gains the support and energy of those past and present members of tradition spiritually. It can make the journey, spirit contact with the gods and healing more effective. Yet without any freedom in the process and space to have your own experiences, the process can be dogmatic, stifling life force, creativity and, ultimately, spiritual growth. The lack of imagery, symbols and guidance can leave new practitioners wandering aimlessly, without clear goals, contact, support or protection. A balance must be sought.

The journeys of this book seek to find that balance for practitioners, rooting the working in the imagery of the Celts, with the intentions of working with the Morrighan in her various forms, but at the same time allowing freedom for your own experiences and the forging of a unique relationship with the Goddess.

Get into a comfortable position. Candles and incense that can appropriately add to the mood of a magickal imram are appropriate. Western magickal traditions often light a black candle to the left and a while candle to the right, creating a gateway for magickal working and journey, but a single candle of either color would also be very appropriate. Mood music can also set the tone, particularly of a Celtic background, ranging from traditional Irish music to modern neo-Celtic and inspiring New Age music. For those seeking a more freeform shamanic journey, rather than a guided journey, a fast, solid drum beat is excellent. Recordings of the Celtic drum known as a bodhran, with a double beater, is a great way to attune to the energy of the Celts while doing this work.

Close your eyes and breathe deeply. Relax your body. Bring your awareness to the top of your head and give your head and neck permission to relax. Give your shoulders and arms permission to relax. Relax your chest and back. Relax your abdomen. Relax your hips. Relax your legs, all the way down to your feet. Feel waves of relaxation move through your body. As you breathe in, count slowly to three. Exhale to the count of three. As you continue, you can change the internal dialogue from a count of three to the three syllables "Mor-Ri-Ghan" on the inhale and exhale to attune to her energy.

As your breath and internal mantra bring you into a deeper state of awareness, imagine yourself floating down a river. The river supports you. The river sustains you. As you float along it, at times you feel it is the most pure, most powerful river on Earth. Other times, you imagine yourself floating down a river of stars, as if in the Milky Way, surrounded by the blackness of space.

In the distance, you see a small bit of land in the river. The river widens to an ocean as you approach the land, and there, growing larger, is an island, with beautiful green rolling hills upon it. As you draw closer, you see three ladies standing upon the island in white, red and black.

You find yourself drawn by the currents of the water to the island, and immediately drawn to the ladies. They surround you. One gives you beautiful clothing, dressing you magnificently, beyond your wildest dreams. You feel like royalty. Another gives you the finest of foods. Anything you love to eat, particularly from your childhood, she has in plentitude and gives to you. The third lady sings to you, a soft lullaby tune that you half remember from your early life. It brings you comfort and joy.

The ladies show you a hill with a doorway in it, a mound from a time past. Through the gate you see a flickering blue flame and they invite you into the interior of the green hill. They guide you inside and enter with you.

As you go deeper into the mound, you feel strange. It is as if the ladies have merged with the walls, and that you too are merging with the mound. You are one. There is no separation. There is no divide, just variations of the one Earth, the one Universe. As you merge with the ladies of the emerald isle, you are shown the world. Your mind races from one land to another, one continent to another, and you feel a oneness with all the streams of life—human, animal, insect, vegetable and mineral. All are like cells within your body, within her body. Everything is feeding everything else. Everything is caring for everything else. It is glorious and beautiful. It's like the secrets of the world are being revealed to you. You feel yourself reaching out to the Sun, planets and stars. They are your kin. Suddenly everything seems connected in a way that makes sense.

Through this connection you find intense light and energy. The light leads to darkness. In the darkness you feel the sensation of floating, and as your vision comes to you again, you find yourself floating along the river, as if you were going full circle and coming back to where you began.

When you reach your starting point, be aware of your breath and body. Feel your fingers and toes. Take three deep inhales and one large exhale. Open your eyes and return your awareness to the world. If you feel lightheaded, take a few moments to regain your composure, or have a little bit to eat and drink, as digestion will bring you back to your bodily awareness. Turn off any music. Extinguish your candles and incense. Journal about your experience.

CHAPTER TWO
The Three Sisters

The mystery of the Morrighan can better be explored through understanding the three who are one. While many goddesses can be included in the Morrighan's trinity, we shall focus on the triad of Badb, Macha and Nemain. These three have been the most prominent in my own experience, and have qualities separate from the overarching associations of Anu/Danu.

BADB

While all the goddesses associated with the Great Queen Morrighan are associated with crows, Badb is the aspect most seen as the crow goddess. Badb's name means "crow" and her title Badb Catha translates to "battle crow" as she was specifically seen as the crow on the battlefield, causing confusion to bring victory to her favorite side, and picking over the fallen soldiers in the battle, partaking of the carcasses. Battlefields are known as the "land of Badb" to the ancient

Irish. She spreads the news of battle victory in the form of a crow, and did so after the battle with the Fomorians. The Gaulish deity surviving in a single inscription, Catubodua, shares the same translation as battle crow and could possibly refer to the same goddess. Badb is also a term for sacrificial victims, so between the battlefield and the sacrificial associations, Badb is a goddess of violent death.

Her name has also been linked with rage, fury, poison and violence, as well as faeries, Witches, demons and specifically the bean-sidhe, or banshee, the faery specter warning of death. The banshee could appear in the form of crows, cawing out their warning.

While Badb's mother is Ernmas, like her sisters, her father is said to be Delbaeth.

Delbaeth is the son of a Tuatha (either Ogma or Aengus) and a Fomorion, the daughter of Balor, Ethniu. Ethniu also went on to give birth to the god Lugh, with whom the Morrighan goddesses have a strong relationship. Like Lugh, this dual ancestry of Tuatha and Fomorian shows they are deities standing between, being neither wholly of order and light or chaos and darkness. Within them is the potential balance and the necessity to bring things to balance. Perhaps this is why many of Badb's, and by extension, the Morrighan's, actions are not always comprehensible. It can be hard to see whose side she is on, for she is on the side of cosmic balance, not personal loyalty.

Delbaeth also fathered the land sovereignty goddesses Ériu, Banba and Fodla. They too stand between the worlds and embody a higher order, though perhaps they embody more gentle aspects of sovereignty, where the goddesses of the Morrighan embody war and violence, that which must be forcibly removed to bring prosperity to the land. While it's hard for us in the human realm to understand, such forces are more akin to harvesting and weeding, taking what has matured and must move on, and removing that which doesn't serve, to make room for new things to grow. Such forces are necessary if not pleasant.

Her husband is known as Neit or Neid, with whom she shares with Nemain. Most would then assume she is the same figure as Nemain, and while they share so many similar characteristics in the Morrighan trinity, they are said to have two different fathers. This suggests they are two different goddesses.

While she is given such specific familial connections, denoting an individual, the name Badb would also come to signify a group of battle goddesses, not just a specific entity, much as the Morrighans, Morginas, or Morrigu is used as a collective term for several entities, not just a single individual deity.

Badb is a sorceress, a Witch. She casts powerful spells beyond the simple charms common in the Craft today. In the First Battle of Moytura, against the Fir Bolgs, Badb, along with Macha and Morrigan, rains down her showers of sorcery and blood. Again the three raise "pillars" of stone to prevent anyone from leaving the battlefield.

Badb is also a prophetess. She is a seer with visions of the future, and relates them to her people. At the end of the Second Battle of Moytura, after the defeat of the Fomorians, it appears that Badb gives a two-part prophecy. She gives bright prophecy of time ahead, but ends with a song prophesizing the end of the world. Like most references, it's hard to distinguish the actions of the Morrighan from Badb, or if Badb is a title for the Morrighan in the various translations.

Then after the battle was won and the slaughter had been cleaned away, the Morrigan, the daughter of Ernmas, proceeded to announce the battle and the great victory which had occurred there to the royal heights of Ireland and to its sid-hosts, to its chief waters and to its river mouths. And that is the reason Badb still relates great deeds. "Have you any news?" everyone asked her then.

"Peace up to heaven.
Heaven down to earth.
Earth beneath heaven,
Strength in each,
A cup very full,
Full of honey;
Mead in abundance.
Summer in winter. . . .
Peace up to heaven . . ."

She also prophesied the end of the world, foretelling every evil that would occur then, and every disease and every vengeance; and she chanted the following poem:

"I shall not see a world
Which will be dear to me:
Summer without blossoms,
Cattle will be without milk,
Women without modesty,
Men without valor.
Conquests without a king . . .

Woods without mast.
Sea without produce. . . .
False judgments of old men.
False precedents of lawyers,
Every man a betrayer.
Every son a reaver.
The son will go to the bed of his father,
The father will go to the bed of his son.
Each his brother's brother-in-law.
He will not seek any woman outside his house. . . .
An evil time,
Son will deceive his father,
Daughter will deceive . . ."

— *Cath Maige Tuired.* Translated by Elizabeth A. Gray. Stanzas 166–167.

When looking at the end of the prophecy, one might be tempted to see our current world in those words with environmental and political decay. It's hard not to look at the prophecy and see a possible admonishment of homosexuality, though technically it is specifically a prohibition against incest. One can wonder how the first prophecy, with a bright outcome can turn so sour. A variant translation of the prophecy ends the "bright" prophecy with the phrase "be this nine times eternal." Eternity is no longer eternal, though Neopagans might see this second prophecy as influenced by the Christian scholars of the time of the recording, echoing the "end time" prophecies. A truly Pagan Celtic woman, by all accounts, was probably not described as "modest" either. Yet other Indo-European cultures, such as the Norse, have their own end time prophecies, like those of Ragnarok. Looking at the prophecy with a Neopagan slant, some think of the "evil time" as the rise of Christianity in Ireland.

Boa Island is named after Badb, translated to Badb or Badhbha's Island. It is the largest island in the Lough Erne lake of Northern Ireland, and upon it are carved stones, an enclosure and a graveyard. Most notable are the two anthropomorphic stone statues. Both are considered Pagan deities and one is bilateral, divided. Many have described it as Janus, the two-faced god of the Romans, but it is not literally a depiction of Janus. It simply shares archetypal qualities with the god. The figures are assumed male, but could as easily be goddesses, considering it's the Island of Badb.

It's common amongst many modern and ancient Pagans to look for equivalent deities in other cultures, particularly the classic Greeks and Romans. While the deities are not equivalent as spiritual entities, it proves useful in two ways. What figures, and what proves useful? It helps us to understand how those making the comparisons understood that goddess at the time of the writing, as well as help to inform our own experience and understanding as mystics. Badb has been equated with a variety of classic figures, including the Greek Fury Tisiphone, as the word Badb became synonymous with "fury" at one point.

Tisiphone's own name means "avenging murder." She is one of three Furies, or Erinyes, whose name means either "angry ones" or renamed the Eumenides, the "kindly ones." These deities were born out of the drops of blood that struck the land when Cronos castrated his father, the sky god Uranus. They are goddesses of vengeance, depicted with wings at times, or with serpents upon their head, like Medusa and the gorgons. Tisiphone specifically punished crimes of murder, and could use the snakes from her head to exact her vengeance. Due to these associations, the snake-haired Medusa was also a figure connected with Badb.

Badb is linked to the Roman war goddess Bellona. Bellona is believed to be an early native Etruscan deity, and was considered a relative of Mars, either as wife, sister or daughter. She is depicted as a fierce warrior dressed for battle.

Badb's name also became synonymous with the Caileach, the Irish and Scottish Crone of winter.

The crow goddess has much to teach us in understanding the nature of the Morrighan, from battle to sorcery, prophecy to venom, each illuminates a different aspect of our complex goddess.

Invocation of the Battle Crow

Badb
I call to you.
Badb Catha
Battle Crow
I call to you.
Badb Catha Morrigu
Battle Crow Queen
I call to you!

Daughter of Ernmas
Daughter of Delbaeth
Wife of Neid
I call to you now.
Bringer of Fury
Grant me success in my battles.
Avenging Lady
Grant me justice
Prophet Crow
May your calls lead to wisdom and success
Nine times eternal!
So mote it be.

MACHA

Of any of the goddesses associated with the Morrighan, Macha is my favorite. Perhaps it's because her presence is so strong in my life. I feel she really chose me and put me on my path after my initial exploration into Witchcraft, but I think it's also due to her having such a powerful and distinct presence in the literature. Her stories have the most "meat," and I'm sure she would have it no other way.

Macha's name usually translates to "field," "plain" or "pasture," demonstrating her connection to the sacred land directly, as well as her association with grazing animals. While the Morrighan is associated with crows, Macha is specifically related to horses as one story demonstrates her speed and endurance to outrace a horse. This has led to speculation in connections with other horse-related goddesses, including the figures of Epona and Rhiannon. Yet her crow association should not be played down, as the term for a flock of crows, the molmacha, contains her name. I often refer to crows as machas in my rituals and my daily life. So did my mother.

"Epona" Horse

One of the amazing aspects of Macha, also spelled Mhacha or Machae, is her various distinct incarnations. While one would argue as a goddess she is immortal, she seems to take divine, semi-divine and even mortal forms in the world, making her akin to the Hindu concept of an avatar of the Morrighan. An avatar is the physical incarnation of a higher cosmic deity in the world to usher in a new teaching or age. I think the Pagan world in general would be aided by looking at some of our figures in the light of the avatar teachings of the East, including Macha and the Italian figure of Aradia. Such thinking could help us understand better the blurry lines between gods and mortals in Celtic myth, and better understand how our own divinity incarnates in flesh, in our lives here and now.

Macha is described as a triple goddess herself, with three more famous incarnations, but she has at least five historical manifestations. Perhaps they are all incarnations of the same entity. Or perhaps Macha is just a beautiful and powerful name carried on by five different entities. While we don't assume everyone with the name John is the same specific soul, there is an underlying thread of myth and history connecting all of the five Machas.

The three popular incarnations of Macha are the wife of Nemedh, the wife of Crunnchu and Macha Mongruad, Macha of the Red Tresses. Interesting how two of the incarnations are defined by her husband, and could possibly relate to the Morrighan's function as the sacred queen of the land and bestower of sovereignty. The other two incarnations that are not cited as popularly are primarily identified with her parents: Macha, daughter of Partholon, and the Macha of the Tuatha de Dannan, daughter of Ernmas.

Macha Daughter of Partholon

The earliest recorded incarnation of Macha is the daughter of Partholon. In Celtic myth, Ireland is invaded several times and settled by various races ranging from the seemingly human, human and the somewhat monstrous. Partholon is the leader of the first settlement after the great flood, as recorded in *The Bible*. While the first to arrive in the classic invasion lore, they were in actuality the second to arrive in other renditions.

It's possible she is also the second Macha in our cycle, while this Macha's fate is never revealed, and she plays a little role in the story of this "invasion." It is believed that all of Partholon's followers, except for his nephew Tuan, died of the plague in a single week. Tuan was the one to preserve his story, surviving through a series of amazing animal transformations to be reborn with his memory intact, living to repeat and share the history of Partholon.

Interestingly enough, in the tale of Partholon as told by Seathrún Céitinn, there is a seemingly male Macha named as one of his "strong-men" along with Mearan, and Muicneachán.

Macha Wife of Nemed

The second Macha is the wife of Nemed. Nemed succeeded Partholon as the leader of the next wave to inhabit Ireland. Nemed, or Nemedh, means "sacred one." We believe he is an ancestor to the Tuatha de Dannan. This Macha was said to prophesize the destruction coming to Ireland in the time of the Tuatha de Dannan during the battles with the Fir Bolgs and Fomorians, and this vision broke her heart and literally killed her. She was the first of his people to die in Ireland—another tie to link her to the health and happiness of the land of Ireland itself. Sources disagree as to whether she died twelve days after their arrival or twelve years, though interestingly enough, the use of twelve, an astrological number, due to the twelve signs of the Zodiac, is associated with her death. Nemed buried her in a field, giving it the name Ard Mhacha, or Macha's High Place, which became Armagh. It's found in Northern Ireland, a place well known for its association with Macha, and for strife and violence between the Catholics and the Protestants. Perhaps this is the origin of her name in association with fields.

Macha of the Tuatha de Dannan

The third Macha is the one most associated with the Morrighan. She is seemingly one of the Tuatha de Dannan, daughter of Ernmas. It is this association that cites her as a Morrigna. This also begins her association with crows through these raven women. Of all the Machas, she appears to be the most divine. Though the immortality of the Tuatha de Dannan is often in question, she seems to most certainly be a goddess.

The third Macha is also the most bloodthirsty of the Machas. Like Badb and Nemain, she incites battles and instigates fights. Severed heads upon the battlefield were called "Macha's acorns." The Mesrad Machae, or Macha's Mast, is another term for this "acorn crop." Strangely the use of the acorn nut gives a subtle link to the oak tree and the ancient caste of Druids. The severed heads were on the field of battle, the "crop" of an open pasture, fed by the blood of fallen warriors, giving us another interesting link between the land and the battle. One could see such victims of battle as a form of tribute and sacrifice to the Earth goddess. Perhaps they point to an earlier sacrificial practice.

This Macha was a sorceress, able not only to prophesize, but rain down fire and blood as well as move stones with her sisters. She seemed to prize the head above all else, and in the Celtic worldview, the head held the power or the soul of the enemy. Head hunting and skull practices were a large part of Celtic magick, both in honoring an enemy and gaining power. In this way, you could possibly compare her to the psychopomp figures of the Norse Valkyries, yet no mention is made of her leading the souls of the fallen warriors to a hall of eternal feasting and reward. If this was ever a part of her myth, I would imagine it would be exorcised from the later Christian renditions. But because of the deaths instigated in battle, and her collection of heads, she can be perceived as a death goddess or underworld goddess presiding over the land of the dead. In the Celtic worldview, the land of the dead was not such a terrible place. One could even make Indo-European comparisons of Macha with the severed heads to the Hindu Kali, bearing a necklace of skulls and a skirt of severed arms.

While she could be the figure to continue onward as our fourth Macha, it is said that she was killed by Balor along with her husband Nuada in the second Battle of Moytura, though their deaths like many other gods, do not seem so permanent. Folklore says this Macha, or at least one of the Machas, was killed by St. Patrick and the rise of Christianity in Ireland, during the Thirteenth Battle of Bismarck. Evidently she was too dark a goddess to be converted into a saint like Bridget.

Macha Wife of Crunnchu

The fourth Macha is the faery wife of Crunnchu, also Cruinn or Cruinniuc. Her story is probably the most complete and well known of all the Machas. Crunnchu was a widower living in

Ulster. Macha, described as a faery woman and daughter of Sainrith mac Imbaith, the strange son of the sea, mysteriously appears to him one day and begins keeping his house in silence. She joins him as his wife, and for as long as they are together, his wealth increases. This is another acknowledgement of her role as goddess of sovereignty As she is honored, the land, or household, prospers. When she is not, there is trouble. She ritually enters his bed at night, turning deosil, or Sun wise, before entering. To move clockwise (Sun wise) is a symbol of the power of growth and health. It is a magick to increase and prosper, as opposed to the movement against the Sun, widdershins, which decreases, hexes or enters the mysteries of the dark. Soon after her arrival, Macha becomes pregnant by Crunnchu.

Ulster holds a great assembly, a gathering of sports and games, and Crunnchu decides he wants to go. Macha warns him never to speak of her. She must remain a mystery, but he doesn't listen to her warning. He watches the king's chariot race, and boasts that his wife is faster than them all. Crunnchu must have either witnessed some of Macha's supernatural talents, or inferred her status as an otherworldly woman with her strange rituals and his increase in wealth. King Conchobar mac Nessa hears of Crunnchu's boast and is insulted. Crunnchu is brought before him, and the king demands he prove his claims.

Macha is summoned to the king and agrees to race, but requests it be done after her pregnancy has come to term. The king refuses. She announces that she is Macha, daughter of Sainrith mac Imbaith, and warns the people of Ulster that a great evil will befall them all because of this. The king still forces her to race. She does so, and easily beats the horses, justifying the boasts of her husband, but as she crosses the finish line, she cries out in pain and gives birth to her children, twins, right upon the spot. In her cries, she curses the men who hear her, and their descendants unto nine generations, to suffer her labor pains for five days and four nights in the time of their greatest need. Only women, small boys and their descendant Cu Chulainn, who is an embodiment or avatar of Lugh, would be immune.

The spot where she gave birth is referred to as Emain Macha, or Macha's Twins. It's not far at all from Armagh, another historic Macha site. Now called Navan Fort, it has become a place of power and authority for both the Catholic and Protestants. St. Patrick based his operations near Emain Macha, perhaps believing to establish himself in a center so strongly associated with a Pagan goddess, yet continuing the "great evil" predicted by Badb/Morrighan when the goddess is disrespected by men in power.

As this Macha predates Cu Chulainn, cursing his people, and Badb, Nemain and Morrigan are all existing in the time of Cu Chulainn (despite potential earlier deaths by the Fomorians), she could be the same as the third Macha, of the Tuatha de Dannan, simply reappearing. St. Patrick's invasion comes far after the rise and fall of Cu Chulainn. The involvement of King Conchobar, as semi-historical figure, would date this story around the first century B.C. But the third Macha never references a father of the sea, and the fourth Macha never references Ernmas, so they could be different and entirely separate "incarnations" of Macha. The timeline of Macha we find in a pseudo-mythic history that is difficult to conform to a linear progression.

Macha Mongruad

The fifth Macha is Macha Mongruad. Her name means "Macha of the Red Tresses" or "Macha of the Red Mane," again with a horse implication. This incarnation is the most human and historic, yet in many ways, the most powerful as well. Even in one aspect of her story, her humanity can be brought into question due to her implied stature. She is a Queen of Ulster, and the only queen listed in the List of the High Kings of Ireland.

She was the daughter of Aed Ruad, who shared kingship with his two cousins Dithorba and Cimbaeth for seven years at a time. After his third term as king, Aed drowned. When it was Aed's turn again, rather than simply divide the kingship among the two remaining, Macha claimed the kingship for herself. The men refused to let her be Queen, and a battle began. We again see the theme of women denied their rightful place of respect in Ulster. Macha wins, and Dithorba is killed. She was challenged by Dithorba's sons, and defeated them until they fled into the wilderness to plot against her again. She married Cimbaeth and shared kingship with him, cementing her rule.

To neutralize the threat of Dithorba's descendants, she hunted them down in the wilderness alone. Macha disguised herself as a leper, and strangely, was able to subdue each of the men in turn. This aspect of the story is somewhat reminiscent of the Goddess Sovereignty, appearing as a hag and offering to kiss or to have sex with various knights. All refuse her but one, and that one is granted kingship. Macha Mongruad, however, doesn't offer them kingship, but enslavement. She comes across the five sons roasting a pig and joins them for dinner. One by one, she makes her advances and takes them out into the darkness. She seduces them, quickly defeats them, ties them up and carries them off. Single-handedly she neutralizes this threat to her rule. While her people want them killed, she instead forces them to build a fortress stronghold for her.

Macha marked out the large boundary with her broach pin, leaving some to believe that she must be rather large, and carry a large pin, as it was implied she simply marked the space around her without getting up. This would put Macha Mongruad in a similar status of giant or titan with the Dagda, the Morrighan of the Fomorian battles and the Welsh Bran the Blessed. For this reason, Emain Macha is sometimes referred to Eomuin Macha, or "Macha's Neck-Brooch."

Macha of the Red Tresses ruled with her husband for seven years, until he died of the plague, and then ruled fourteen years on her own. She was killed by Rechtaid Rigderg. His father, Lugaid Laigdech, was killed by Macha's father, Aed Ruad. He was then killed twenty years after by the foster son of Cimbaeth and Macha, Ugaine Mor.

This Macha's reign is dated by various sources as around 323-283 B.C. (Lebor Galbala), 468-461 B.C. (Foras Feasa ar Eirinn) and 661-461B.C. (Annals of the Four Masters). While all of these histories would predate the fourth Macha in our list here, Macha Mongruad seems the least connected to the faery women and sorceresses of the Tuatha de Dannan, and the most human and political.

While continuing the association with Ulster and with battle and sovereignty, she has the most complete history and genealogy, and is considered to be at least a semi-historical figure listed in the history of kings. The various invasions of Ireland cannot truly be dated, as we cannot look at the Fir Bolg, Fomorians and Tuatha de Dannan as historic figures any more than we look at Zeus, Cronos and Uranus of the Greeks as historical figures, even though we have some suspicions of various early arrivals to Ireland upon whom these mythic peoples could be based. If they are names of enfleshed ancestors, their historic stories are left in the gray mist of mythos. We presume the first three Machas' dates live to be found in mythic pre-history. The fourth Macha, while dated, is obviously an otherworldy visitation. She may continue the themes of the Macha of the Red Tresses, and even be an aspect of her return to the men of Ulster.

This fifth Macha is more rooted in history, and unlike the previous Machas, the most likely to take direct action. While the previous incarnations prophesize and rain down sorcery, instigate battle, fly as crows, collect severed heads and curse the men of Ulster exacting retribution, Macha Mongruad claims queenship for herself and battles to keep it. She is a fierce warrior and a trickster. She uses cunning and guile, as well as sexuality. The only potential connection to otherworldliness is tenuous at best, with her potential stature and carving out of the boundaries of her fortresses.

Invocation to Macha

Macha of the Red Fire Mane
Macha of the Black Feathered Cloak

Macha of the Green Burial Field
Be with us.

Daughter of the Sea
Tender of Dreadful Acorns
Faery Queen
Be with us.

Macha, Mother of Twins
Macha, Seer of the Future
Macha, Lady of the Red Tresses
Be with us.

Grant us your blessings.
May we heed your warnings
And always honor you as Goddess and Queen
Blessed be.

NEMAIN

Nemain, also Nemon, has a few meanings to her name. Usually it is translated as "panic" or "frenzy" referring either to the panic she stirred upon the battlefield in her enemies, as she would shriek fiercely to intimidate others and cause them to drop dead with fright by her primal battle cry, or the frenzy she stirred in the blood of her allies. The northern tradition's warriors, both Celt and Teuton, were well known for their fearless battle fury against the more regimented Romans. Celtic battle was much like Celtic society, fierce and loosely structured when compared to the Romans.

Like Badb, she was considered a prophet, yet it appeared her prophecies were the imminent death caused by her shrieking, or the results soon after. She could cause confusion, fear and death with her sound. This cry gives her a very clear connection to the Bean Sidhe, banshee, the faery whose wailing portends death.

Another translation relates Nemain's name to "venomous" giving us another connection to Badb, and her Medusa/Tisiphone connection. The results of her cry were certainly venomous in spirit, if not a literal poison. Modern linguists look at the popular venom link to Nemain and find it suspect. While the Proto-Celtic word "nemi" relates to "dealing out a dose of poison" and is the origin of her venomous translation, popular thought now relates her name to a Proto-Indo-Eurpean root "nem," without the "i" root, meaning to "sieze, take, deal out." Nem is the root word also connected to the Greek goddess Nemesis.

Nemesis is a goddess of justice and divine retribution. Today we think of a Nemesis as the ultimate enemy, the foil who is like the hero, but also the opposite of the hero, but originally Nemesis simply meant to distribute fortune, good or ill. Though appearing a bit more personal and judgmental than its eastern counterpart, karma, this notion is similar nonetheless. It's the result of your actions. When personified as a goddess, Nemesis tends to particularly punish for the sin of hubris. Strangely she was also linked to Aphrodite, and the more familiar goddess of love and sex would carry the epithet Nemesis. While our concepts of love/sex/attraction and justice/punishment seem to be two separate concepts, embodied by two separate deities, it is easy to see them united in the world of the ancient Irish Celts through the figure of the Morrighan. While perhaps the etymology is speculative, with other theories giving her names such as the "Great Taker" or "Great Twister," the mystical connection between Nemain and Nemesis can be quite enlightening.

Invocation of the Frenzy

Nemain
Nemain
Nemain
Primal panic,
primal blood.

Nemain
Nemain
Nemain
Venom filled
Nemesis

Nemain
Nemain
Nemain
Shrieking Cry
Twisted One.

May there always be peace between us
So mote it be.

Like Badb, Nemain is married to Neit, and is referred to as Neit's wife more than Badb is. *The Book of Leinster,* while listing at one time Badb as a wife of Neit, also lists Nemain and Fea, and Nemain and Fea are sisters who share the same lineages, so perhaps they are the same goddess. Nothing else is really known about Fea beyond her associations with Nemain.

Like Badb, Nemain's mother is usually considered the mysterious Witch goddess Ernmas, but her father is Elcmar, who is the Son of Delbaeth. The Book of Leister goes on to give his lineage as the son of Ogma, son of Eletan. Stranger still as Elcmar is often considered to be a guise of Nuada, the first king of the Tuatha, who led the battle against the Fomorians until losing his hand and abdicating to Lugh. Nuada was the husband of the third Macha.

Badb and Nemain were said to be slain by Neptur of the Fomorians, yet like many of the Morrighan's characters, they seem to come back unhurt in later stories, particularly those in the hero's journey of Cu Chulainn.

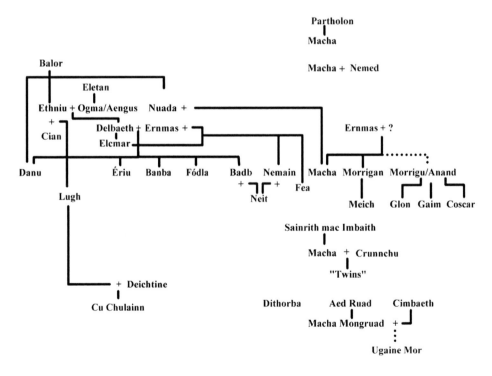

Genealogy of the Morrighan

Though not connected in the classic literature, many Neopagans, myself included, see links between the triple goddess of the Greeks, such as the Furies and the Fates, as well as the Norse Norns and Saxon Wyrd Sisters, with the triplicity of the Morrighan. She seems a force beyond the gods themselves, changing the course of history not for her amusement or ego, but for the proper order of the world. In the Teutonic and Greco-Roman cultures, even the chief gods themselves, often thought of as omnipotent by the masses, were not immune to fate and fury.

JOURNEY TO THE THREE FACES OF THE GODDESS

As with the last journey, set the mood and get into a comfortable position. Lighting three candles of the traditional triple goddess colors—white, red and black—would be appropriate. Close your eyes and deeply breathe, relaxing your body. You can chant internally the name of the goddess, "Mor-Ri-Ghan" as you do to align yourself with her mysteries.

Again with time the flow of your breath reminds you of the tides, in and out and you are moving upon water. Rather than take you to an island, the flow of the dark water brings you into the darkness of a cavern.

The cavern is illuminated with small bits of glowing material, like a phosphorous lichen, bright enough to see, yet still veiling the realm below in shadow.

Your craft reaches land and you find steady ground within the world of darkness and get out, led by tiny lights. The lights take you to a warrior woman, sharpening her blade. Clad in red, she is Badb Catha, the Battle Crow. She is the prepared warrior, and the prophetess. She welcomes you and asks you your plans of battle and your plans of life. What do you tell her?

She grabs your hand sharply, and reads your palm, predicting your fate in the battle of life.

When done, she ushers you back to the phosphorous light, a light that guides you onward in the dark.

A second figure appears to you. Clad in a black feathered cloak, with streaks of red braided in her otherwise ebony hair, Macha awaits you. Which Macha is it? Macha of Partholon? Macha of Nemed? The great sorceress Macha of the Tuatha de Dannan? Macha of the Twins? Or Queen Macha Mongruad?

Macha holds something in her hands that you cannot see. She turns to show you, and it's your own severed head, your own acorn of Macha. She presents you with it to face your own mortality. Like her, you will have many incarnations, but each will come to an end. That is the only promise she has. All that lives must die. All that dies has lived. All comes from the land and will return to the land. All feeds the pasture gardens of the Goddess.

Take this time to speak to the goddess Macha, the goddess of the dark feathered cloak, about life and death.

And again, when done, she sends you forth on the luminous path.

The luminosity starts to gather and take shape, forming a figure of eerie white light. The lady of white is Nemain, the lady of the fearful frenzy. She begins to wail and cry, and it strikes at your very blood. What you fear comes up within you. What are you afraid of? What do you hold back from? What drives terror in your heart and makes you panic? What is the poison you carry with you? She reveals it to you.

As you face your fear, her scream turns upon it. She helps you break it down. It becomes small and less significant. You take control of it and understand it better. You are able to master the fear, rather than it mastering you. She quiets from her frenzied rage and speaks to you of your fears.

Her light breaks down, like the fears, and guides you back, as you realize you've walked full circle back to your vessel, to journey upon the water again. You enter the boat and ride upon the water, exiting the cave.

You surrender to the rhythmic tides in and out. The in and out of the sea, of your breath, and of the cosmos. Feel your awareness return from the water to your body and breath. Feel your fingers and toes. Take three deep breaths and exhale strongly. Open your eyes and return your concentration to the world around you. Ground yourself as necessary and journal about the experience.

Chapter Three

The Faery Queen

While strict Celtic reconstructionists will insist that the Morrighan of the Irish myth cycle has absolutely nothing to do with the Morgan of Arthurian myth, they have nonetheless become linked over time. Much like the various Morgan goddesses strictly speaking have nothing to do with Tisiphone or Bellona, yet at some point in their history they have been linked to gain better understanding, we are now living in one of those points of comparison.

It's an obvious connection to make, when looking at the names. Morrigan, Morrighan, Morrigina and Morrigu are not all that different sounding from Morgan, Morganna and Morganna Le Fay. Technically considered to come from two different roots in two different branches of the Celtic language, with the Morrighan coming from Irish Gaelic and Morgan drawing from the Welsh.

Morgan is Welsh for "sea dweller" or "born of the sea," though as a name, usually refers to a male. That's quite different from the "Phantom Queen" of the Morrighan, though many still suspect there is a link phonetically. Morgan has been referred to as "Sea Queen," giving a closer parallel to the Morrighan. When Macha refers to herself as the daughter of Sainrith mac Imbaith, strange son of the ocean, there is a link to being a "sea dweller" even though that Macha is not specifically depicted being in or near the ocean.

While the figures of Arthurian myth might be transformations of native Welsh deities, no figure similar in name and form to Morgan is found in Wales predating her first mention in Geoffrey of Monmouth's writings. He is responsible for the start of our familiar Arthurian and Avalonian lore, though his original writings bear little resemblance to our pop culture understanding of them.

Author August Hunt, author of *The Secrets of Avalon*, makes the argument that Geoffrey placed variations of Irish goddess who were well known to him at the time in place of native Welsh ones that were not, depicting nine sisters on the sacred isle of apples. Chief of these sisters is Morgen/Morgan, who is chief healer among her sisters, and taught them the arts of astrology, giving rise to the idea that she is a sorceress and can prophesize the future. Curiously, she can shift her shape, and take flight with wings, though the type of wings are not described. It's easy to imagine her as a crow or raven. Hunt proposes specific Irish goddesses as cognates for the nine sisters of Avalon. The sisters are named as such:

Morgen

Moronoe

Mazoe

Gliten

Glitonea

Gliton

Tyronoe

Thiten

Thiten cithara notissima (or Thetis)

While two separate cultures, the Welsh and the Irish are not as separate as one might think. Many of the myth cycles, while different, appear to have linguistic cognates, and journeys and adventures span all of the British Isles. Bran the Blessed battles the King of Ireland for the honor of Bran's sister, Branwen. The gigantic description of Bran, a titanic force, often earns him comparisons to the Irish Dagda. The original Cauldron of Regeneration in his tale was said to make its way to Wales with a couple from Ireland. There is also a Bran in Irish mythology, found in *The Voyage of Bran*. The Welsh Lleu is compared to the Irish Lugh or Nuada. The Irish Manannan mac Lir has an obvious connection to the Welsh Manawydan fab Llyr. The Irish Danu is compared to the Welsh Don. Welsh-to-Irish comparisons are not without merit. Even the concept of Avalon itself could rise from Irish myth, which bears a mysterious land to the west, Tir na Nog, also associated with many lands even further west.

The work of modern Goddess teacher Kathy Jones names the Goddess of Avalon the reflection of the name itself in the waters of the lake—Nolava. Her tradition is rooted in Glastonbury and she is the co-founder of the Glastonbury Goddess Temple and the Isle of Avalon foundation. In her work, the nine sisters are placed around the Neopagan wheel of the year with other magickal correspondences. Here are some of the associations from this tradition with the nine sisters:

Tyronoe	Winter Solstice	North	Air	Sword	Wren, Eagle, Owl, Buzzard
Thitis (Thiten)	Imbolc	Northeast	—	Spindle	Swan, Snake, Cow, Wolf
Cliton (Gliton)	Spring Equinox	East	Fire	Wand	Bear, Hare, Hen, Cat
Thetis	Beltane	Southeast	—	Comb, Mirror	Mare, Horse, Dove, Swan
Gliten	Summer Solstice	South	Water	—	Dolphin, Whale, Salmon, Seal
Gitonea	Lammas	Southwest	—	Chalice, Loom	Dear, Stag, Horned Creatures
Moronoe	Autumn Equinox	West	Earth	Stone, Orb, Crystal	Boar, Badger, Fox
Mazoe	Samhain	Northwest	—	Cauldron, Sickle, Scissor	Crow, Sow, Toad
Morgen	—	Center	—	—	—

These associations can help flesh out the sparse details of these nine sisters in a Neopagan goddess context, though they come from one modern tradition. If your own interactions with the nine sisters yield different images, go with your own experiences. More of Kathy Jones' teachings can be found in *Priestess of Avalon Priestess of the Goddess: A Renewed Spiritual Path for the 21st Century.*

In our popular Pagan culture today, the depictions of these goddesses are coming closer and closer together. Statues and paintings of one could easily depict both figures, the Morrighan and Morgan, despite the original artists' intentions. You could think of this as due to the lack of research, respect or talent on the part of the artisans, but there is something greater connecting the two in the collective magickal psyche. Gods live, grow and die by how they change in human perception. The godforce itself can be eternal, but the gods' expressions of themselves change over time and worship, as people's relationship and understanding change. There is little consistency in the surviving Celtic mythos of ancient times, so why should modern times be different?

We have to imagine that the gods' relationships with humanity change as the people who worship them change. Today we do not live in a Celtic culture. Many who work with and worship the Celtic gods, particularly through modern Witchcraft, might have little direct contact with anything that would be considered surviving authentic Celtic culture. Celtic culture has changed through immigration, and many of Irish descent are exploring their Pagan roots, often from teachers who do not share the same ancestral background. The gods live in the land, in the blood and in the heart and soul of the people. Change any of these things, and our experience of the gods will change.

My strongest reason for including information about Morgana Le Fey in a book dedicated to the Morrighan is my own experience. The two have blended and morphed in my own visions of the Goddess. As it deepened my Craft experience, I began to have more contact with those of the Welsh and Arthurian mythos, and the prominent role in my spiritual practice usually filled by Macha soon became filled with manifestations first of the goddess Ceridwen and then Morgana, as they shared with me that they were both ladies of the lake. Morgana appeared as healer and herbalist, brewing potions on the apple island, but she would have a feathered cloak and be surrounded by crows and ravens. On a pilgrimage to Glastonbury, the reputed site of Avalon in the physical world, while upon the Tor itself by St. Michael's Tower, I had a very profound experience with a crow, flying into the wind and surfing the breeze to remain eye to eye with me for over ten minutes. I felt in contact there with both Morgana and Macha, and that the two often inhabited the same psychic space, giving me further thought to the links between these figures.

My understanding of the Goddess in general, and the Morrighan in particular, is much more universal than most, and on that trip I made peace with trying to figure out either/or, and saw them as together when they appeared together in one form, blending traits to and fro. My philosophy is to take the living gods as they come to me, and not to try to make them conform to the earlier cultural images when they themselves don't want to conform. It doesn't mean I ignore the past lore, but I realize that it might be the earlier chapters of a deity's own evolution, and we're in a new section of the story. My philosophy has resulted in some strange visions including Anubis in a leather jacket and Gwydion in a three piece suit, but thus far it has yielded perennial personal success.

MORGAN THE FAERY

The strongest mythic link Morgana shares with the Morrighan in traditional lore is that of the Faery. Her title Morgana Le Fey, Morgana the Faery, shows that she has an otherworldly connection. Her various stories either emphasize or hide her connection to the otherworld. Our most familiar modern Arthurian tales depict her as almost entirely human, an evil and scheming Witch bent on destruction. Yet in the earliest tales, she is simply depicted as a faery woman, living on the isle with her sisters.

The faery connection to the Morrighan is not as apparent to most people. Today, we tend to think of Faeries as small winged creatures flitting from flower to flower. Yet that is not the traditional understanding of faeries. In the tales of the Tuatha de Dannan, rather than battle the Milesians and risk destroying their beloved isle, the Tuatha de Dannan make a duplicate of their world within the land, a mirror image, and retreat to the depths. They are referred to as gods, and later faeries, the bright and shining people of the land. While there is a variety of races of spirit beings within the land, and some tiny and flittering, that was not the dominant image of faeries until the last two hundred years or so. Faeries are otherworldly creatures connected to the land and nature, but just as likely to be tall and majestic as small and insect-like. They are great magicians, healers, artists and warriors, and the rules of human society do not apply to them. So the Morrighan in all her aspects is said to dwell within the land, the body of the Earth in general, and Ireland specifically. She is a faery being.

Another popular image of Faery land was not beneath the land, but beneath or below the water. Still water holds the perfect reflection of the world, and was considered a gate to the realm of the Fey. Others saw it beyond the western ocean, the western sea as a metaphor for the unknown, the realm of the dead and the realm of mystery. Many cultures placed their mythic lands in the western sea, giving rise to tales of Atlantis, Electra, Hesperdies, Tir Na Nog and Avalon.

So Morgen turned Morgan le Fay, Morgan the Faery, shares these connections with the Tuatha, though she too, is never stated to explicitly be a goddess.

Morgana the Fate

While there is a wide range of associations today with the term faery, including nature spirits and elementals, Pagan gods, spirits of the dead and fallen angels, the origin of the word relates to the concept of fate, from the word fata, a personification of the Fates. Fate refers to the divine force that guides, or even perhaps rules, your life. Many cultures have the concept of fate as personified, the most famous being the Greek Moirae, the Roman Parcae, the Norse Norns and the Wyrd Sisters, or Three Witches, of British Pagan lore. While the Moirae and Parcae were always numbered three, the Norns were numerous, though three have gained prominence. Sometimes the fate goddesses are considered weavers and spinners of destiny, and other times caretakers of the tree of the world, but they are personifications and custodians of a primal force that governs the cosmos, and specifically, human lives.

Faeries were at one time agents of fate. Perhaps not for these specific entities in Pagan lore, but when we look at their surviving folklore, their capricious nature of doing things on a whim, or doing things that will advance the story of the myth, which is often to instigate trouble rather than placate the humans, we can see agents of fate. I was taught that Faeries are an elder race with their own code of behavior in tune with the laws of nature above the laws of man. They have their own society, and politeness and respect with them always does us well, but they do as they must, not as we would desire, unless we are in harmony with nature. The more in harmony with nature we are, the more we do as necessary, like the faeries, rather than fulfill the desires of ego.

When we look at the agents of Fate, of faeries, in that light, we can catch a glimpse of the Morrighan. The most popular fate deities are "triple" much like the Morrighan herself. They often cause strife, as the Morrighan often causes battle. They don't do as they are bidden, but follow their own elusive agenda. The Greek Fates are described as having jurisdiction even over the gods such as Zeus. No one, divine or mortal, is free from their influence. The Morrighan influence the battles of the gods, of the Tuatha de Dannan and the Fomorians and Fir Bolgs, and then over humans in the story of Cu Cuhulainn. The Fates, and the Morrighan, seem beyond the motivations of both gods and mortals, and work within the scheme of nature and super nature.

The first literary depiction of Morgen of Avalon (or Affalon), the Isle of Apples, appears in the work of Geoffry of Monmouth. He was the first to write what he claimed was a British folkloric history drawn from other, now lost, sources. He wrote *The History of the Kings of Britain*, as well as *The Prophecies of Merlin* and *The Life of Merlin*, introducing us to the familiar characters of Arthurian romance in their earliest incarnations.

The first incarnation of Morgana La Fay was Morgen and her nine sisters. Nine is three times three, an interesting association when looking at links with the Morrighan. She is usually depicted as a triad of goddesses, but there are far more in her mythos: Morrigan, Badb, Macha, Nemain, Fea, Anu/Annan/Danu, and possible Ériu, Banba and Fodla. Though she has many more associations and guises, these "core" Irish identities amount to nine, though they do not easily link in any way with Morgen, Moronoe, Mazoe, Gliten, Glitonea, Gliton, Tyronoe, Thiten and Thiten Cithara Notissima, as far as I can ascertain beyond Morrigan and Morgen. They were simply the mystical women of the apple isle, healers and magicians. This Morgen receives Arthur at the end of his mortal life for healing, so he may return as the Once and Future King.

One can perceive of this Morgen as the fabled Lady of the Lake, though she is not directly described as such. She is one of the benevolent faerie ladies. In later stories, the Lady of the Lake, under various names, is a benefactor to Arthur and Merlin, granting the famous sword Excalibur, which, contrary to popular story, is different from the sword in the stone. Excalibur is a sword of light and truth, and the scabbard prevents its wearer from bleeding. In many ways the scabbard is more important than the sword itself, but both tools grant the user an immense advantage over the standard odds of battle. The scabbard, like the cup, is a sign of feminine power, healing and restoration.

MORGANA THE VILLAINESS

The image of Morgen is split, divided for literary sake, into a "good" character and a villainess, an evil character. The good becomes the Lady of the Lake, often renamed Viviane, or Nimue, though she too is divided, and sometimes becomes both lover and enemy of Merlin the magician, trapping him away in a cave, tower or tomb.

The malevolent becomes Morgana La Fay in various incarnations. Her faery nature is hinted at, but she becomes all too human, motivated by jealousy and malice. Morgana takes on many attributes in this human guise that are akin to the actions of the Morrighan. Much like the

Morrighan seems to be an indirect enemy of gods and warriors, though in the end might be spurring them onto greater deeds, Morgana becomes the enemy of Arthur. Themes of sexuality are found in both stories, with almost a love-hate attraction between the two. She births his bastard son, Mordred, who will be the final blow to the seeming paradise of Camelot. She steals Arthur's scabbard, and plots his overthrow. Yet without her machinations, it's possible that the knights would not have sought out the Grail and began the quest to restore and redeem the wasteland.

His Queen, Guinevere—in the later version of the tale, seemingly "good"—also plays a role in the downfall of Camelot through a betrayal with his best knight, Lancelot DuLac, or Lancelot of the Lake, the adopted son of the Lady of the Lake, another faery being. Some considered Guinevere, usually depicted as human, as an aspect of the Goddess of Sovereignty, of Brigitiania, the British equivalent of Ériu, the lady of the land, and therefore another faery woman. All these faery beings and faery-touched humans are bringing down the kingdom, but perhaps they unknowingly, even to the authors of the story, have a higher purpose as agents of fate?

The Morrighan, Phantom Queen, can also be seen as the Faery Queen, for in the world of the ancient Celts, the realm of the Dead and the Fey are not so far away from each other. Some believe the Faeries are the souls of ancient humans interred into the land. The myth is later transformed into the Christian era, when the tales of the Morrighan were written, to mean that faeries were the souls of unbaptized children, or fallen angels who didn't quite side with heaven or hell, so they only fell half way. Such an understanding of the spirit world broadens our understanding of the Phantom Queen. The Morrighan has dominion over all manner of spirits, including the agents of fate.

Today the Morrighan is favored by Witches, and many believe the dark-cloaked Druidesses in the most ancient accounts of the Celts are women emulating Morrighan-like figures to incite fear in the heart of their enemies. While they may not necessarily be worshipping Morgana Le Fey, she has become an archetypal figure or spiritual ancestor many modern Witches emulate and honor. Her archetype was seeded into the modern occult movement through the novels of Dion Fortune, particularly her heroine of *The Sea Priestess* and *Moon Magic*. Taking the name Vivian Le Fey Morgan, and later Lilith Le Fey in the sequel, the adept character is a reincarnation of an Atlantean Sea Priestess possibly inspiring the legends of Morgana Le Fey in her ancient lives. Many popular fictions and occult lore connect the legends of Atlantis with Arthurian mythos.

Many Witches today also see the secret Goddess of the Witches, the Queen of the Universe, as the triple goddess of fate, the Weaver. Our rituals of initiation make us "free from fate" as Traditional Witchcraft teacher Robert Cochrane once said, as we move in harmony with her, with what is necessary, rather than what we personally desire. Perhaps our draw to the Morrighan is an expression of this great goddess of necessity.

Call to the Nine Sisters

Morgana of the Waters
Morgana of the Isle
Morgana of the Faery Folk?
Open the Way to the healing waters
Open the Way to the flow
Open the Way to the Mysteries
That dwell deep below.
Morgan of the Nine Sisters
Chief among them all
Stand in the center
Of the Wheel of Eight Spokes
And stand tall.

Moronoe stands at the Western Gate
Bearing the fruits of the land.
Mazoe stands at the gates of life and death
Sickle in her hand.
Gliten rides the summer waves
Calling the creatures of the deep.
Glitonea works the straw loom
As we sow we shall reap.
Gliton holds the fire
From the Star of the East
Tyronoe walks the North Star Road
And prepares the solstice feast.
Thiten prepares the baby's bed

Fit for the sleeping king,
Thetis kindles the fires of Bel
For all to dance and sing.

Morgana of the Waters
Morgana of the Isle
Morgana of the Faery Folk?
Keeper of the Mysteries
Keeper of the King and Child.
We welcome you.
Blessed be.

THE RITUALS OF WATER

As Morgana is often considered a type of water faery, a nymph or sprite, albeit a powerful one, in this form of chief sister on the isle, we can learn from the spirits of water. Water can heal. Water can reveal. Water can be a gateway to other realms, a portal to new horizons of consciousness. When honoring and working with the spirits of water, what many magicians call undines or merfolk, we can have access to these blessings. Morgana, as a powerful spirit connected to water, both the pure water of springs and lakes and the mysteries of the western, or Atlantic, ocean, can commune with us from any source of water.

Start with an offering to the spirits of water. Water that has been altered, possibly enhanced if we can be so bold, is an appropriate offering. Water is perfect on its own, but the best offerings to spirits are those offerings the spirits cannot acquire on their own. Offerings picked directly from nature do not have the effort and love of human hands. That is why often breads, cheese and alcohol were traditional Celtic offerings to the faeries. They require human effort upon natural substances. Teas, or infusions, of water with appropriately suitable water herbs can make an excellent offering to rouse the attention of the water spirits. Take a few pinches of any of the following—mugwort, jasmine, willow or lemon balm—and add 1 cup of boiling water. Let it steep overnight. If the Moon is full, let it steep under the light of the Full Moon and take it in before day break. If possible, add a piece of sterling silver jewelry, for silver is the metal of the Moon and the element of Water, or even better, a few drops of colloidal silver found at most health food stores. When cool, you can preserve it by adding 1/3 of the volume of the brew with a high proof, clear potable alcohol, such as vodka or grain alcohol.

When ready to do this working, find a suitable pool of water in nature. Ideally it should be still, though I've had great success with very slow moving bodies of water, such as the bends in streams where the water pools. Others like to gaze into the distance of the ocean. Traditionally it is done under the light of a full or nearly full Moon, but I've also had success in working with Sunlight reflected off the water.

Pour out your offering and ask for the presence of the water spirits. You can even use the previous evocation poetry of Morgana of the Waters. Hold an intention. Do you seek healing? Do you seek to scry, to have a vision to answer your questions about your life and path? Do you seek spirit contact? Do you seek to journey into a spirit world, and if so, where? Become clear in your intention.

Sit and gaze into the reflected light off the water. Allow the energies of your intention to rise up and come through the water. If you chose healing, healing energy may flow from the light into your eyes, into your energy centers and shine through your aura. You might find yourself filling up with this water energy, like a glass filling with water. If you seek knowledge, the light may swirl and take shape, clear or cloudy, answering questions about your life. Spirits might show their faces in the pool, as if under the water, or even in your spirit vision rise up and out of the water to commune with you. Or the water will open up and allow you entry into the spirit world. If you journey, call upon Morgana to guide and protect you in the journey.

When done with your experience in the realm of water spirits, bring your awareness back to your flesh and blood, breath and bone. Feel your body. Feel your fingers and toes, wrists and ankles. Take three deep breaths and exhale out strongly. Open your eyes and return your concentration to the world around you. Thank the spirits, particularly the spirit of Morgana, who can move through all forms of water. Ground yourself as necessary and journal about the experience.

CHAPTER FOUR

The Goddess of the Land

While I personally think of the Morrighan in all her guises as more grand and universal, not limited to one location, one cannot deny the plethora of evidence relating her directly to the land of Ireland. Yet, I do think the various mythic invasions of Ireland are more universal than one country, and speak of a greater metaphor of the coming and going of more cosmic ages of mythic races upon planet Earth. Ireland is the world and the world is Ireland in these myths. Ireland is simply the point of reference for those of Ireland to understand themselves in relationship to everything else. It becomes the center of the universe. So the Morrighan is of Ireland, but is also of the world and universe itself.

In ceremonial circles, we would call an expression of this idea the Principle of Correspondence. "As above, so below. As within, so without" is the familiar phraseology. Ireland is what is seen and known, and is the microcosm. The world, the cosmos, the great macrocosm, is reflected in this one land. You can see this principle played out among the Irish, in myth and in government, as the land is divided by both practical and sacred proportions, imitating a pattern of ritual that is found all over the world in relationship to sacred space.

The Emerald Isle

Ireland is divided into four provinces. Today they are known as Connacht, Ulster, Leinster and Munster. Basically the land of the emerald isle is divided into realms of the four directions. The Irish word for the division of the land is cúige, which means "fifth part." Meath was once considered the fifth, but was incorporated into Leinster and Ulster. Yet there is still a secret, sacred fifth part to be found within it spiritually, no matter how the lines are drawn today.

Each of the kingdoms was magickally associated with an aspect of the culture and tradition according to old Irish traditions.

Connacht

Connacht is the western kingdom. It is associated with education and learning, and the traditions of magick and the wisdom of Druids, the Celtic priests and magicians. The mythic magickal lands are often believed to be found off the western shore. Those living in Connacht are considered eloquent and wise, being able to discern good judgment. The flag of Connacht is divided vertically, with half of a black griffon on a white background on the left, and a white hand and dagger on a blue background to the right.

Ulster

Ulster is the northern kingdom. Its magick is one of battle and valor. Here are the mightiest warriors of the land, though it is also an area associated with strife and death. The flag of Ulster is yellow-orange with a red cross. In the center of the cross is a white shield with a red hand.

Leinster

Leinster is the eastern kingdom. The quality of the eastern land is abundance. While all of Ireland is hospitable, here you find the greatest hospitality. It is the realm of prosperity and good fortune, often due to the rich imports from the eastern lands. The people of Leinster are refined and beautiful. The flag of Leinster is a golden harp on a green background.

Munster

Munster is the southern kingdom. This is the realm of creativity, particularly of music and art, but also skilled masters of sports and talented horsemen. The greatest fairs and gatherings occurred in Munster. The flag of Munster is blue with three yellow crowns.

Meath

In the center of them all is the hidden kingdom of Meath, the realm of the steward of the land, the king, ruling from the Hill of Tara. The Hill is the traditional high seat for the High King of Ireland. The flag of Meath is a king on a throne seated on a blue background.

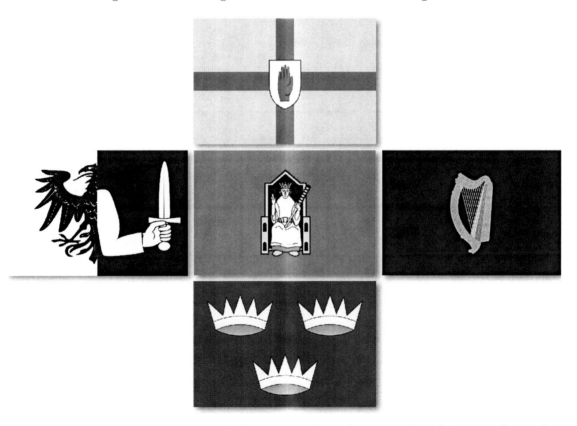

Flags of Ireland: Ulster (top), Connacht (left), Meath (center), Leinster (right), Munster (bottom)

Any occultist begins to see the potential for modern elemental associations with the five provinces. The elements of both western and eastern magick refer to four states of being reflected in four forms of nature. These states of being refer to the energy of the universe, the energy within ourselves and states of consciousness we carry. They are associated with a whole host of common and magickal correspondences, and are one of the keys for understanding magick and spellcraft. The most tangible representation of these forces in nature comes in the form of fire, water, air and earth.

Fire is the energy of creation. It is associated with passion and drive, as well as battle, anger and violence. Water is the element of emotion. It deals with our relationships and feelings, as well as the astral plane, where our passions and ideas first take creative shape. Air is the element of the mind, of thought and language. It is the mental plane of existence, where everything exists as a potential idea. And earth is the element of manifestation. It is the physical plane, where all takes form and lasting shape. It is the body and the resources of the physical world. Spirit is the fifth mysterious element. The four spring from it and return to it.

Ulster	North	Fire	Warrior, battle
Leinster	East	Earth	Abundance, prosperity, beauty
Munster	South	Water	Creativity, music, art, horsemanship
Connacht	West	Air	Learning, magic, eloquence
Meath	Center	Spirit	Kingship, stewardship, sacredness

Perhaps only water with Munster is not as obvious a correspondence, as the southern kingdom is not associated with death, nor love and healing, but the expression of emotion is a creative act, and therefore within the realm of water. Since the elements can be subjective, other associations can, and have been, suggested.

It's important to realize these are the associations of modern occultism and the Neopaganism influenced by it. The Irish themselves didn't have the western four element system (or the Chinese five element system, for that matter) but knew the elements in nature's poetic mix of earth, sea and sky with flowers, trees and clouds. Their divisions were not as sharp as the European alchemists' or Greek philosophers'. Perhaps that's why it's not a perfect match, but it does help us to understand the patterns we, as modern magickal people, see them as today.

THE FIVE GODDESSES OF THE LAND

Three goddesses, three daughters of Ernmas, are most strongly associated with Ireland specifically: Ériu and her sisters, Banba and Fodla. Ériu is the name whence we actually derive the word Ireland. These three sisters are linked to the various faces of the Morrighan. In some instances they are siblings, sisters or half-sisters. In others, they could be one in the same. It appears that the work of Seathrún Céitinn (Geoffrey Keating) was the first to explicitly name the triad as the same, or perhaps suggest that the three land goddess "worshipped" the three war goddesses.

Eire and Fódhla and Banbha, three daughters of Fiachaidh, son of Dealbhaoth, son of Oghma. Eirnin, daughter of Eadarlámh, mother of those women.

Badhbh, Macha, and Móirríoghan, their three goddesses.

Right away we have an association of the land with the goddess, or in this case, goddesses. And these goddesses have a more overt or easily seen side with the goddess of the land who meets and marries with the invading Milasians, and a mysterious and enigmatic side found in the Morrigu.

When you explore the folklore and traditions of each of the Irish provinces, and in fact, with every county and even village, different figures are emphasized beyond these two triads. The living land is rich with the stories of Pagan goddesses and gods and tales of older times and ages. Goddess and Celtic scholar Patricia Monaghan outlines her study and experiences of the Irish goddesses in her book, *The Red-Haired Girl from the Bog: The Landscape of Celtic Myth and Spirit*. In it (and the workshop I was lucky enough to take with her at a festival) she outlines five major goddesses associated with the provinces of Ireland, and the sites where each can be experienced through a relationship with the land.

Ulster	North	Macha	Armagh
Leinster	East	Brigit	Kildare
Munster	South	Cailleach	Cliffs of Moher
Connacht	West	Medb	Knocknarea
Meath	Center	Ériu	Uisneach Hill

The warriors of Ulster continue to play a strong theme in our journey with the Morrighan. Here we have the only truly explicit manifestation of the Morrighan in this vision: Macha. There is no doubt that Macha is the matron goddess of Ulster, and of course Armagh. All her various forms have some association with the northern territories where she had made her home.

The goddess strongly associated with Leinster is Brigit, also known as Brigid, Bridget or Brid. While she is beloved by all of Ireland, it is in Kildare where she is most strongly associated. Brigit is also beloved by modern Pagans and celebrated in the Wheel of the Year on her festival day of Feb 2, or Imbolc. She is considered the goddess of poetry, healing and smithcraft, and in particular associated with fire and water. With the coming of Christianity, Bridget worship could not be stamped out, so she was eventually adopted into Christianity and changed into St. Bridget. It's even possible the story of St. Bridget was based upon a high priestess in the shrine of the goddess Brigit in Kildare, and adapted to help convert the Celts to Christianity.

At first glance, Brigit has no direct link with the Morrighan in any of her guises, but she is related to one of the gods most strongly associated with the Morrighan, the Dagda. Brigit is the daughter of the Dagda, according to *The Book of Invasions*. The mother is never named. While we know that the Dagda and Morrighan mated across the river the night he sought to gain a victory plan over the Fomorians, we would assume that Brigit was already born and fully grown, arriving with the Tuatha de Dannan when they appeared on the shores of Ireland. Yet nothing in the tale of the union of the Morrighan and the Dagda states it was the first time together. While pure speculation, it's possible the Morrighan is the mother of Brigit, as poetry and prophecy are not far off in the mind of the ancient Celt. When we think of the Morrighan and her connection to Danu, the mother of all these gods, it is not a far reach to connect them.

Brigit has two sisters, both named Brigit, making her a triple goddess in her own right. She has three main areas of dominion, and some would see each sister ruling over one aspect—poetry, healing and smithcraft. While they all seem somewhat separate and disjointed to us today, all three are arts, and all three require special knowledge and inspiration to perform correctly.

She is associated with the flame of inspiration, the hearth and the forge, but she is also strongly linked to water, and the healing wells that bear her name. In a sanctuary devoted to St. Bridget, nineteen nuns tend the eternal flame in her name. While this manifestation occurs today in the context of a Christian tradition, the concept of a priestess order tending a flame is found in many Indo-European traditions of the pre-Christian era. Bridget also has a holy well dedicated to her in Kildare, where the water is associated with healing miracles. Clooties, or cloths tied with prayers to the trees near the well, connect the pilgrim's wish, prayer or "spell" to her.

In many ways, Brigit is the antithesis of the popular thoughts regarding the Morrighan. She is bright while the Morrighan is dark. Her magick is of creativity and healing, fire and water, while the Morrighan is the land itself and the destructive powers of war and justice. Brigit was adopted by the Christian church as a saint, while the Morrighan was associated with the lamia, specters, goblins, nightmares and the demon mother Lilith. Yet in their opposition, there is a connection. Each must contain a bit of the other. With creation comes necessary destruction. With destruction comes the chance at renewed creation. While not popularly associated with the land in the mind of most Neopagans, Brigit is intimately connected with the landscape of Ireland, the green being the "mantle of Brigit" particularly retold in the popular story of the Earth Shapers from *Celtic Wonder Tales* by Ella Young, a modern interpretation of the Tuatha de Dannan stories, that strangely omits the Morrighan.

In the southern territories of Munster, we have an aspect related to the Morrighan as the Old Woman, the crone or Cailleach. Her name means "old woman" and can also refer to a "veiled" or "cloaked one" with some references to the old Witch archetype. She appears in Irish and Scottish myths, as well as on the Isle of Man. Her figure is so old, many debate her nature. Is she the first woman? The creatrix? Mother Earth? Or a deified ancestor of the most ancient people to inhabit the British Isle? We don't know, as her origin could be any or none of these theories.

Cailleach shares some of the darker crone attributes with the Morrighan. She is the frightening old woman. Named Cailleach Beare in Ireland, or the "shrill" hag, she is described as blue skinned and one eyed, with long red teeth and matted dark hair. She is associated with the land itself. The hills and mountains were said to have fallen from her apron, or have been created as her stepping stones. For this she is seen not only as an Earth goddess, but as she who creates the Earth, a creatrix of a more universal variety. She is also known as the daughter of the Grianan, or little Sun, the Sun of the waning year, as she embodies the withering season, as mother winter. Her staff freezes the ground as she walks. She herds deer, gathers firewood and creates storms.

Mountains and crags are manifestations of the Cailleach in the land. She is particularly associated with Ceann na Cailleach, or the Hag's Head, on the southernmost tip of the Cliffs of Moher in the County Clare. In west Cork, she is linked with the Beare peninsula as well as the island Inis Boí. There a rock in the water is named the Cailleach's great bull, or Tarbh Conraidh. This bull was so great that merely its bellow would impregnate other cows who heard it. He went swimming after a cow, and the Cailleach struck him with her staff and turned him to stone. Interestingly, one of the animal totems of the Morrighan is the Cow.

She shares a special relationship with the goddess Brigit, as some versions of her tale depict her undergoing a miraculous transformation at the end of winter. Either she becomes a stone boulder, no longer traveling the land and inducing winter, or she reaches a spring of youth, and drinking from it, is turned into a bright maiden of spring and life, considered to be an aspect of Brigit. The tale is very similar to the images of the goddess simply known as Sovereignty.

Sovereignty would appear to men as a horrible hag, and ask for a kiss, sex or marriage. For the lucky man who respected and even cherished the horrible hag, she would transform into a beautiful maiden and offer kingship of the land, for a king must respect both the land and all women to rule wisely. Sovereignty has obvious parallels to the Ériu and to the aspects of the Morrighan. The Cailleach's association with Sovereignty is particularly strong in Cork and Kerry, in the province of Munster.

Medb, also known by the Anglicized Maeve, is the goddess of Connaught. In the Ulster Cycle of myths, she is the Queen of Connaught, and emphasizes a woman of power and sexuality, becoming the enemy of the men of Ulster, akin in many ways to Macha, mother of the twins. She is the former wife of King Conchobar mac Nessa, the king of Ulster. The marriage was arranged by her father, and she left him to return to Connaught, eventually instated as queen. Conchobar raped her at a gathering at Tara, initiating a war between Ulster and the High King. Medb insisted her husband have three traits. He must be without fear, without meanness and without jealousy, as even when married, she had many lovers and children. She asked a Druid which of her sons would kill King Conchobar. The Druid named "Maine," a name that none of her sons possessed, so she renamed all her sons with "Maine" somewhere in their title.

She had many husbands, and insisted upon equality with them in terms of power and wealth. Her desire to equal her husband King Ailill, who owned a powerful bull, one more than her, resulted in her theft of a prize bull from one of Conchobar's vassals. Thus began the legendary Cattle Raid of Cooley.

Medb's name is considered a cognate to the word mead, and roughly means "she who intoxicates." The tales of her sexual appetite and her fertility through numerous children makes us speculate that she is no mortal, but a goddess, like the various Goddesses of Sovereignty. Mead is also the sacred drink used in marriage ceremonies, and would be part of the ritual link between the sacred king, as leader of the people, and the queen as embodiment of the land.

Her place of rulership is Cruachan in the county of Roscommon, though it is better known today as Rathcroghan. She is said to be buried in a stone cairn in the summit of Knocknarea in Sligo County of Connacht. In her grave she is upright, facing her enemies in Ulster. She also has strong ties to the land and history of Mayo.

Queen Medb is also curiously connected to the faery queen of Shakespeare, Mab. Though a diminutive creature entering the brains of people to change their dreams, she drove a chariot like a warrior goddess. As Macha and the Morrighan have both been considered faery ladies, or faery queens, it creates an interesting connection to Medb for our consideration of the Morrighan.

In the center we have Ireland herself, Ériu. Where else would you expect to find her but in Meath? She is particularly associated with Uisneach Hill in Westmeath. It is the magickal center of Ireland, what was known in Greece as the omphalos, or the stone in the center of the world, the great naval stone. While traditional science claims the stones of Stonehenge to be from Wales, a folk tradition says that the stones come from Ireland, and it was from this spot they were taken. At Uisneach, the provinces were said to come together. Here the great celebration of the whole nation took place, particularly Beltaine. Mide, a Druid of the Nemedian invasion, lit the first fire of Ireland there. The fires lit on Uisneach could be seen at Tara, and then those gathered on Tara would light their celebratory fires. It is upon this spot that Ériu receives her promise from the Milesian bard Amergin to give the country her name.

THE LAND AND THE MORRIGHAN

While the goddess in her many forms can be seen all over the myths, place names and culture of the provinces of Ireland, the Morrighan can be specifically found across the land as well. Though Ulster is her strongest region, not just for her associations with the Morrighan, but due to the Tuatha de Dannan myths that focus on the region, she can be found in other places. By honoring the lands she has touched, you honor and understand her better.

Ulster

In Northern Ireland, there are several sites sacred to the Morrighan in the form of the goddess Macha. Armagh, from Ard Mhacha is Macha's Height or Macha's High Place. Today it is a medium-sized town classified as a city in the county of Armagh, with a strong association with Christianity, though it has a long history of Paganism associated with it.

St. Patrick is usually associated with Armagh, as he made his first church there and decreed that only those who studied in Armagh could spread the Gospel. But long before St. Patrick, the place was sacred to the goddess Macha.

Armagh is the resting place of Macha, wife of Nemed. After her prophecy about the war between the Tuatha de Dannan and the Fomorians, along with the destruction it would bring, she perished. Nemed buried his lady in the field and named it Macha's High Place.

Nearby is an area believed to be a Pagan worship site, though in the myths of Macha, it was where she gave birth to her twins. It is also where Macha Mongruad, before that sacred birth, measured out her fort with the pin of her brooch. Emain Macha is now known as Fort Navan, though it's not really a fort, but archeology seems to show it as a ceremonial site. The evidence discovered by scientists does not yet seem to support the magick and mystery associated with the land. It played a major role in the Ulster Cycle of Irish myths. Emain Macha was the capitol of the people known as the Ulaid. From their name we get the name of the land Ulster. The kings found in the tales of the Ulster Cycle were related to the Ulaid.

West of the city of Armagh, the site of Emain Macha is built on a hill, forming a circular enclosure surrounded by a bank and a ditch inside the bank. Due to the construction, it does not appear to be built to be secure militarily. Various artifacts and constructions can be dated to the Bronze Age and Iron Age. One of the strangest was the skull of a Barbary Macaque monkey, obviously not native to Ireland, but Algeria and Morocco. In the records from the Annals of the Four Masters, Emain Macha was said to be burned by the Three Collas (Colla Uais and his brothers Colla Fo Chri and Colla Menn) in 331 AD after defeating the King of Ulster, Fergus Foga, in the battle at Achadh Leithdeirg. Archeological evidence shows that it was deliberately burned down and then covered by a mound of earth, similar to that of the Tara site.

The Bed of the Couple, where the Dagda and the Morrighan united on the River Unius, is located in Donegal.

Tireeworigan in Macha's territory of the county of Armagh means Land of the Morrighan.

Leinster

In the county of Louth there is a field of the Morrighan known as Gort na Morrigna. According to the Book of Fermoy, her husband the Dagda has given the field to her. In the county of Wicklow, there is the Crich-na-Morrigna, as mentioned in the Book of Lismore. Beyond that, not much is known about this site.

Munster

Twin Hills near Killarney, County Kerry, in the providence of Munster are known as the Paps of Anu, or Dá Chích Anann or the Breasts of Anu. Anu is associated with various spellings of Ana, Anann, Anand, Aine and of course Danu, and through all these names, the Morrighan. While we traditionally associate the Morrighan with death and war, the figures associated with the Paps of Anu focus on the goddesses of fertility and abundance. Breasts are obviously associated with the powers of sustaining life through nourishment. She is a goddess of cattle, caring for the people and teaching the arts of dying wool and clothing, though as a goddess of cattle, she was also responsible for the culling of the weak. Like the traditions of never calling the Fey by their name, but as the Gentle Folk, she is referred to as Gentle Annie. During midsummer celebrations, fires would be lit in her honor.

Also in Munster is Fulacht na Morrigna, the ancient "cooking spot" also called Morrighan's Hearth, found in the Country of Tipperary. The Morrighan had a cooking spit with three magickal pieces of food—raw meat, dressed meat, and butter. It was said the raw meat would be dressed, the dressed meat could not burn and the butter, even when it was in the fire, would never burn.

Connacht

Connacht doesn't have a specific terrestrial incarnation of the Morrighan as we know her today in the land, though interestingly enough, it was in this province that Nuada allowed the Fir Bolgs to choose to settle after their defeat. Perhaps this isolates the western province in some way from some of the Tuatha influence.

Meath

The Da cich na Morrigna is the Breasts of the Morrighan, like the more well known Paps of Anu. The breasts of the Morrighan are found near New Grange in the County of Meath. Mur na Morrigna is the Mound of the Morrighan found in the Boyne Valley.

Ulster	North	Macha	Armagh, Emain Macha
Leinster	East	Morrigna	Gort na Morrigna, Crich-na-Morrigna
Munster	South	Anu	Dá Chích Anann, Fulacht na Morrigna
Connacht	West	—	—
Meath	Center	Morrighan	Da cich na Morrigna, Mur na Morrigna

The Four Fabled Cities

The four provinces in the microcosm of Ireland, real and marked upon maps, can find some correspondences with cities not found on any map in the larger, mythic macrocosm. They are simply known as the "four cities" of Irish Celtic myth, and have played a powerful role in modern Neopaganism and Witchcraft. They first appear in the story of the Tuatha de Dannan.

According to the account of The Second Battle of Mag Tuired, the Tuatha de Dannan studied in four cities, with four wizards or sages, in the Northern Isles.

The Tuatha De Danann were in the northern islands of the world, studying occult lore and sorcery, Druidic arts and Witchcraft and magical skill, until they surpassed the sages of the Pagan arts.

They studied occult lore and secret knowledge and diabolic arts in four cities: Falias, Gorias, Murias, and Findias.

From Falias was brought the Stone of Fal which was located in Tara. It used to cry out beneath every king that would take Ireland.

From Gorias was brought the spear which Lug had. No battle was ever sustained against it, or against the man who held it in his hand.

From Findias was brought the sword of Nuadu. No one ever escaped from it once it was drawn from its deadly sheath, and no one could resist it.

From Murias was brought the Dagda's cauldron. No company ever went away from it unsatisfied.

There were four wizards in those four cities. Morfesa was in Falias; Esras was in Gorias; Uiscias was in Findias; Semias was in Murias. Those are the four poets from whom the Tuatha De learned occult lore and secret knowledge.

— *The Second Battle of Mag Tuired* Translated by Elizabeth A. Gray. Verses 1-7

To my knowledge, it is not until the writings of the poet and seer Fiona Macleod (aka William Sharp), that the directions were associated with the four cities.

There are four cities that no mortal eye has seen but that the soul knows; these are Gorias, that is in the east; and Finias, that is in the south; and Murias, that is in the west; and Falias that is in the, north. And the symbol of Falias is the stone of death, which is crowned with Pale fire. And the symbol of Gorias is the dividing sword. And the symbol of Finias is a spear. And the symbol of Murias is a hollow that is filled with water and fading light.

— *The Little Book of the Great Enchantment* by Fiona Macleod

Wind comes from the spring star in the East; fire from the summer star in the South; water from the autumn star in the West; wisdom, silence and death from the star in the North.

— *The Divine Adventure* by Fiona Macleod

These teachings combined give us another set of correspondences to the Macrocosm, and possibly start some of the confusion regarding the "correct" associations of the elements in modern Witchcraft. From this lore, as well as various other associations in European magick, such as the traditions of Mithras, we have the classical Witchcraft and ceremonial magick tools of the stone/pentacle, wand, athame and chalice.

While we must assume that Fiona Macleod was familiar with the older stories of the Tuatha, (s)he obviously didn't agree with the choice of symbols. The biggest confusion between symbols in magick today is between the blade/sword and the spear/wand, and their associations with both air and fire.

Falias	North	Earth	Morfesa	Stone of Fal/ Stone of Death
Gorias	East	Wind	Esras	Spear of Lugh/ Dividing Sword

| Finias | South | Fire | Uiscias | Sword of Nuada/Spear |
| Murias | West | Water | Semias | The Dagda's Cauldron/Hollow |

If you look, you'll find these correspondences differ from those of the four provinces of Ireland in terms of direction. While the north of Ulster is associated with death, as in Macleod's Stone of Death, the powers of the warrior are classically associated with fire. Leinster's abundance doesn't necessarily fit Gorias and the spear or sword, unless you think of eastern wind as bringing change and new blessings. Fire with the south is actually one of the few that fits well with Munster, as creative arts are often described in terms of fire. The learning, magick and eloquence of Connacht is traditionally ascribed to air, the element of learning, not water. And strangely, the cauldron of the Dagda, while a vessel like the classic chalice, normally held food, a symbol of earth. At least we can all agree, even through silence, that the center is spirit.

Ritual Circle of the Four Fabled Cities

You can use the mythology and imagery of Ireland itself and the fabled cities, in the creation of sacred space. In most modern magickal traditions, including Witchcraft, we find a system of opening to the ever-present sacredness through the use of a ritual circle. While in immanent traditions the sacred is manifest in everything, we use ritual to affirm our connection to the ever-present divine, as well as to mark a protective energy for our circle to keep us focused on the work and energies at hand. The circle becomes both a shield and a container, standing between the worlds and existing equally in the spiritual world unseen and the physical world. Any action taken in the ritual space is thereby taking place between the worlds, and has great effect as it can be witnessed and experienced by all worlds and all entities, incarnate or not.

A circle boundary is marked by walking with a sacred ritual tool, usually a double-edged blade with a dark hilt, known as an athame, or a wand of wood, crystal or metal. The use of a ritual sword, staff or even broom would also be appropriate. For those working with the Morrighan, the use of sacred woods from the Celtic tree language, the Ogham, would be appropriate. In particular, wands of blackthorn, hawthorn, willow, elder and yew would be great to connect with the energy of the Morrighan. Also swords and spears are appropriate ritual "weapons" to cast the boundary of sacred space.

A ritual tool for this purpose, be it wand or blade, should be passed through the smoke of sacred incense (See Chapter 5) and then held with intention. Your purpose for the tool should be clear in mind, and through force of will and intention, dedicate the tool for the purpose of directing your energy and creating sacred space.

When creating circle, move around the space you seek to hallow three times, starting in the North and moving deosil (pronounced jesh-il or jed-sil), otherwise known as clockwise or with the Sun's movement, with these or similar words:

I cast this circle to protect us from all harm on any level.
I charge this circle to draw the most perfect of energies for my work here.
I create a space beyond space, a time beyond time, where the highest will,
Sovereignty, reigns supreme. So mote it be.

Many goddess-reverent traditions start in the North as its association is the magnetic streams of energy from the poles of our planet. Traditionally the element of Earth is most often associated with the North, being a feminine element akin to the concept of Mother Earth. The North impetus also aligns us with the North Star, the cosmic nail from which the heavens hang and all is aligned. It's a powerful direction. Other traditions tend to focus on the East for the start of the day at dawn, the rising Sun and the clear breezes that blow in from the East.

As you cast the circle, envision a bright light projected from your tool. Many imagine connecting to the Earth and Sky powers, drawing them into the body, into the heart, and projecting that flow of power through the arm and ritual tool, creating a stream of light, most often bright blue, to make the territory of the circle. Envision a perfect ring of light that will eventually take the form of a perfect sphere as you call the quarters.

The four sacred directions are called, with the fifth in the center, much like our provinces of Ireland. While the ancient Irish did not have the Greek system of elements that modern occultism has adopted—fire, water, earth and air—modern occultists and magicians working in a Neopagan Celtic context, myself included, still use them as connection points with the four directions. Different traditions arrange the elements in different ways, and advocate starting or ending with a particular direction. In my own teaching and trainings, I start in the North to call the quarters, just as I did to cast the circle.

To the North, to the sacred city of Falias, I call to the realm of elemental earth.
I call upon the spirit of earth by the blessings of the wizard Morfesa,

keeper of the Stone of Sovereignty.
Hail and welcome.

To the East, to the sacred city of Gorias, I call to the realm of elemental air.
I call upon the spirit of air by the blessings of the wizard Esras,
Keeper of the Sword of Truth.
Hail and welcome.

To the South, to the sacred city of Finias, I all upon the element of fire.
I call upon the spirit of fire by the blessings of the wizard Uiscias,
Keeper of the Spear of Destiny.
Hail and welcome.

To the West, to the sacred city of Murias, I call upon the element of water.
I call upon the spirit of water by the blessings of the wizard Semias,
Keeper of the Cup of Compassion.
Hail and welcome.

In the Temple of Witchcraft tradition, the four hallows or gifts are named after the principles of Sovereignty, Destiny, Truth and Compassion. We use several different orientations for the elements, but when anchored in the physical world, land and seasons known best in Europe, we use the traditional Golden Dawn correspondences of air in the east, fire in the south, water in the west and earth in the north.

As you call the circle, really let your intuition guide you to feel the four fundamental forces and make contact with the mythic guardians of the past. The natural wisdom and intelligence were said to be the guiding force to train the Tuatha de Dannan. What better allies and teachers could we ask for today? As you attune to them, these teachers can speak with you in ritual, dream and vision working, taking your understanding of the four hallows to a deeper level. You too can learn to "surpass all the sages" in your "Pagan arts" by listening to these inner plane teachers from the four cities.

From this point of the circle, the "working" can be done, be it a meditation or journey, a prayer, consecration of a sacred object, healing, ritual celebration or rite of passage. Any religious sacrament or blessing would be done in the center of this established sacred space.

When done, the circle is released by releasing the four quarter energies starting in the north and moving counterclockwise, or widdershins, against the Sun's movement.

To the North, to the sacred city of Falias,
I thank and release the powers of elemental earth
I thank and release the wizard Morfesa, keeper of the Stone of Sovereignty.
Hail and farewell.

To the West, to the sacred city of Murias,
I thank and release the powers of elemental water
I thank and release the wizard Semias, keeper of the Cup of Compassion.
Hail and farewell.

To the South, to the sacred city of Finias,
I thank and release the powers of elemental fire
I thank and release the wizard Uiscias, keeper of the Spear of Destiny.
Hail and farewell.

To the East, to the sacred city of Gorias,
I thank and release the powers of elemental air
I thank and release the wizard Esras, keeper of the Sword of Truth.
Hail and farewell.

As you release each of the elemental powers, feel them withdraw their influence from your circle. Then release the boundary of the circle by starting in the north and again moving widdershins, unwinding the ritual boundary. Do so either by envisioning the tool "sucking up" the energy of the circle, or by expanding it out infinitely across the universe. You can use these or similar words:

I release this circle into the universe. The circle is undone but not broken.

This simple circle technique can both serve your ritual needs and attune you to the Celtic flow to work more deeply with the Morrighan. See the Appendix for alternating quarter calls, anchored less in mythic topography and more in the familiar place names of Ireland, using Ireland as a microcosm for the sacredness of the world.

For a more detailed understanding of the traditional Witch's Magick Circle, and all the preparatory work for building an altar, obtaining your tools, spell crafting and the religious sacraments of modern Witchcraft and Wicca, I suggest working through the lessons of my book *The Outer Temple of Witchcraft.*

Becoming One with the Land

An initiatory experience of many nature-based mystics comes in the form of what modern practitioners might call Gaea Consciousness, an experience of the living awareness of the planet. Gaea, the Greek name of the goddess of the Earth, and possibly all matter, has become the default name for the planetary entity since the popularity of James Lovelock's Gaia Hypothesis. The hypothesis basically argues for the biosphere being a living entity, including humanity, and has been embraced by modern Pagans and Witches. Pagan elder and modern wizard Oberon Zell-Ravenheart articulated a similar idea in more spiritual terms called the Gaea Thesis in the same year through his magazine *Green Egg.*

The experience itself can come in either a peak of awareness, in which one becomes one with the organism of the Earth, usually in a ritual or meditation setting, or experiences a more continuous awareness of the connection to Mother Earth in everyday life as well as in ritual and meditation. The peak experience can even lead to the plateau of integration of this fact into everyday awareness, creating ultimately a permanent shift in consciousness. Many times entheogenic substances, such as psilocybin mushrooms or other allies from the plant and fungus world, can act as a catalyst in ritual or through recreational use. Many a casual user has come into mysticism due to the effects of powerful entheogens.

While the Morrighan is not usually equated with Gaea as the planetary being, much of our lore shows the connection of the Morrighan with the land itself. If we do not restrict the Morrighan's manifestation to Ireland only, as she works with numerous priest/esses and devotees across the world, then would that land with which she is connected not be the entire world? Occultists already look at the invasion stories of Ireland as the microcosmic patterns for the larger world ages and root races. When we look at Ériu, could we not see an Irish cognate to Gaea? I'm sure the Greeks originally looked to the Greek lands as the manifestation of Gaea. While Pagan people all across the world had names for the Earth Mother, were they not all talking to the same planetary force, manifested locally? Are we, as modern Pagans and Witches also talking to the same intelligence? I think so.

Merging with the land gives us both a connection to the *genus loci,* the spirit of the place where we are, and also a connection with the terrestrial entity known as Mother Earth. Our teachings on the Morrighan can lead us into a deeper understanding of our planetary connection, and the mystical revelation that comes with it. While this ritual is a good start to build such a connection, it can pale to the spontaneous initiatory or entheogenic experiences that can occur with the nature mystic. Clear intention and willed effort are an excellent start to attune to the Goddess of the Land.

As with other workings, set the mood. This obviously works best in a place in nature. Ideally seek a pure place within nature where you will be undisturbed. Though a natural location is great, it's important to know planetary consciousness is planetary, and can be connected with inside or outside, in rural, urban or suburban environments. The ideal natural environment, however, gives us more triggers and opportunities to connect. Often the plants, insects, rocks, trees and dirt awaken and act as teachers in a way that is more vibrant than furniture, carpeting and street lights, though many do experience profound truths from these man-made objects, as they too come from nature.

I suggest casting the Ritual Circle of the Four Fabled Cities to create a sacred space in which to do this working. Once centered and oriented between the four sacred directions, in the fifth, associated with Tara and Ériu, begin.

Close your eyes. Breathe deeply. Relax yourself, starting at the top of your head and moving through your feet. You can chant "Mor-Ri-Ghan" to align yourself with the goddess and enter into a trance state.

Feel yourself getting heavier and heavier. Feel the pull of gravity upon your being. Feel the center of the planet, the iron core heart, calling out to you. Moment by moment, you feel yourself sinking deeper into trance, and deeper into the planet itself. As you sink, your awareness disperses.

Feel your sense of self become not only deeper, but diffuse, as if your awareness can focus on many things at once, rather than attuning to only one thing sharply. You are aware not only of the land beneath your physical body, but the area surrounding it.

You feel things on a mineralogical level. You are aware of the dirt, the stones, the various roots digging deep into your soil. The land is like your flesh.

You are aware of the insects and animals burrowing in the dirt. They are not just burrowing. They are a part of you as well, like a limb extended from the body of the land or an organ within your body.

You are aware of the plants rooted within you: the grasses and trees, the herbs and flowers. All is connected, and they are also connecting you to the light above from the Sun, Moon and Stars. You feel them breathe in and breathe out as your lungs.

You are aware of the fungi and molds. You are aware of the often unnoticed agents of decay and rot, cleaning and clearing the land.

You are aware of the waters flowing upon and in you, or lack thereof.

You are aware of the breezes blowing, and the patterns of weather that also make up your being.

You are aware of animal life upon the land. They too are one with it, even though they move more independently from the rest.

You are aware of any human life upon the land—like you, and also part of the greater whole of which you have become aware.

You are aware of the unseen, the bacterium, the virus, the one-celled creatures.

And you are aware of the subtle energies flowing through you, the lines of the land, the dragon paths that connect all sacred sites, for all is sacred. All is connected. You feel the hum of these lines within and the hum and beat of the heart of the Earth itself. You feel connected to that beat. You are one with it. Become one with it.

When done, you feel the pull of gravity, down and out in many directions release you. Gently you come together whole, discreet, somewhat separate. You feel yourself rise up, out of the land, and back to your body. You become one with your own body, your own flesh and blood, breath and bone again. Yet never forget.

As you feel your awareness fully return from the land, breathe deeply. Take three breaths and exhale out strongly. Feel your fingers and toes, ankles and wrists. Feel all your limbs. Open your eyes and return to the world around you. Ground as necessary into waking consciousness. Remember the experience and try to apply its lessons in your day-to-day life.

Chapter Five

Totems of the Goddess

If the Morrighan is associated with the very land itself, then she is also a part of all nature manifest upon the land, including the animals, trees, plants, stones, and people. She lives in the very blood, sap and mineral structures of our world. She, and her variously associated forms, are shapeshifters, becoming one thing or another, and most particularly taking the form of animals.

Today in popular modern metaphysical lore we call an association of an animal with a person, deity or tribe its totem. Coming from a word originally believed to be of the North American tribe of the Ojibwe, and originally referring to a more tribal clan connection, the word totem has taken a wider meaning in today's culture, often with a much more individualistic tone.

Though it is easy to look at many of the fundamental patterns in Native American beliefs and see similar patterns in the indigenous tribal traditions of Europe, and in particular, the Celts.

In mythologies the world over, particular deities are associated with animals, and an experience with the deities' animal can indicate contact with the deity or a message from the deity for those of that culture. Odin is associated with wolves and ravens. Zeus is linked with eagles and bulls. Venus is linked with doves. Horus is depicted as hawk headed, as Thoth is depicted as ibis or baboon headed. The gods of the Celts, and in particular, the Morrighan, are the same. Her stories show direct association with animals, and she often manifests as these animals. By studying the animal's role in culture, religion and magick, we can better understand the goddess.

Again borrowing from Northern Native American teachings, the spiritual power of an animal is referred to as its medicine. While it might as easily be called its magick, medicine denotes a kind of natural power that restores humanity's "right relationship" with the world, nature and the gods. We sometimes get "dis-eased" by losing our sense of right relationship, and the animal spirits can help restore us. Rituals involving the blessings of a particular animal will convey its particular medicine. Those healers who carry the totem medicine of that animal are best to facilitate such rituals.

While using different terminology, other cultures had similar ideas concerning the power of animals, and their guiding spiritual forms from the unseen world, to aid us. As more living traditions have survived among the native people of America, in whole or part, we have a more direct link to those teachings in terms of potentially knowing what a specific tribe believes about an animal. For the Celts, and other European Pagan people, it can be a bit harder. Our associations with the animals comes from folklore, legend and myth, and our modern conceptions of animal "medicine" from these cultures are influenced by our modern perception of the deities associated with the animals. It's hard to demonstrate how the Celtic view of the Morrighan's totem animals influence the Celts' understanding of the Morrighan, as our modern understanding of the Celts' view on the animals often comes directly from the stories involving Morrighan. For this reason, I think it's good to look at a bit of cross-cultural wisdom.

While I believe that each culture has a unique perspective, the intuitive wisdom of many tribal people often runs in parallel with other tribes in different parts of the world. To see some thought or teaching in many places is not evidence that it is found in all places, but it gives us a foundation from which to speculate, and can prove true for us as modern people, even if we can never prove it as being true for a particular group of ancient people. Today's Celtic practices, even in their most scholarly reconstructed form, are probably very different from ancient Celtic rituals, no matter what we would like to tell ourselves. I think we can capture a mood and essence, and then advance that essence in our own traditions. We are not ancient Celts, so I don't think we should be practicing as such. To immerse ourselves in the worldview of the ancients would require us to turn back the clock and give up much of our modern society to truly "get" it.

So my own understanding of the totems associated with the Morrighan will certainly be influenced by many cultures beyond the Celts and shed a broader light on my goddess and her manifestations.

Crow

Due to its direct association with Badb and the battlefield, the crow can be considered an ill omen in its message, indicating war or at least conflict. But the crow is also skilled in many ways. It is a messenger in the lore, bringing knowledge and news. The crows are cunning and opportunistic, as well as focused on their goal. Crow medicine helps us experience these qualities. During the Roman invasion period of Britain, there seemed to be an understanding between the nature of Crows and Horses, perhaps pointing to the link between the Morrighan/Macha and Epona/Rhiannon. Celtic coins from that period depicted a crow riding on the back of horses. In Scottish folklore one who is "going up Crow Road" is in the process of dying. Life can been seen by some as a battle, so in the end, we all die on the Morrighan's battlefield, or the gameboard, of life.

Roman Coin

In modern and native lore, it is the keeper of "sacred law" who decides what is right and in accord with spirit, not necessarily what humans have legislated as right. When connecting this idea to the Morrighan, the crow represents the natural cycles of destruction and the opportunities that rise from it. The crow is also considered the master of magick and illusion and the keeper of truth. A molmacha, or flock of crows, is said to give oracular prophecy, but only the wisest in the land will understand them all cawing at the same time. The flock name has obvious associations with Macha. The caw of the crow urges us to caw ourselves, to speak our truth to the world. In America, "eating crow" refers to humiliation in being forced to "eat" your own words, so communication continues to be a thread in the lore of the crow.

A popular folk poem, "Counting Crows," traditionally used magpies in the United Kingdom, but seems to focus on crows in other parts of the world. This poem shows the crow's association with omens.

One crow means sorrow,
two crows mean joy,
three crows a wedding,
four crows a boy,
five crows mean silver,
six crows mean gold,
seven crows a secret that's never been told.

Raven

While we tend to think of ravens and crows almost synonymously in magick, they are two similar, but different species. Ravens are also a totem of Morrighan, and one of Ériu's forms was a raven. Ravens are usually bigger than crows, and like crows, are still associated with the battlefield and carrion. They are birds associated with oracular powers. In Welsh myth, Ceridwen's son Afagddu is known as the "Sea Raven." She intended him to be the Taliesin, not her servant Gwion Bach, who accidentally imbibed the potion of inspiration. Unlike the Morrighan, the corvids as a whole, both crows and ravens, are monogamous, though ravens are fairly solitary creatures. Like the Morrighan, however, they are also very loyal to their "flock" as she is with the Tuatha.

Ravens are linked with the Welsh god Bran, whose name means raven. Bran had a cauldron of regeneration where the dead come back to life. While not quite so dramatic, ravens and crows find life in death, feeding off carcasses. For this reason the corvus family, vultures and any other scavengers of the dead are perceived as supernatural beings, able to consume what would poison the rest of us. Due to the death and battle associations, they are considered linked to the realm of the dead, and can act as guides.

Ravens are also associated with Odin, as his two raven cohorts are named Thought and Memory, Huginn and Muninn, and fly out into the otherworlds observing for him. As he is a god of magick, Ravens are traditionally associated with magick, ceremony, mystery and healing. Ravens are the journeyers between the worlds, so they are considered shamanic totems for those who master the spirit journey. They are shapeshifters and messengers, associated with smoke signals in Native traditions. Ravens are also tricksters, sometimes working together, sometimes working alone, to get what they want. In the Cherokee traditions, Ravens are not revered, but reviled, along with the owl. In Greek traditions, Ravens are associated with Apollo and Athena, even though Athena is more popularly associated with the owl. It is interesting enough that both birds have a mixed reputation in the Americas.

Cow

Next to the crow, the cow is probably the most popular animal form our goddess takes. The cow has a strong association with earth mothers—as givers of nourishing milk and meat. Hathor is the Egyptian cow-headed goddess of love, beauty, music and child birth, equated with Venus by the Greeks. In Norse mythology, the great cosmic cow known as Audhumla is one of the primal powers in the creation of the cosmos. In Celtic mythology, in the Táin Bó Cuailnge, much of the story relates to various cows and bulls, showing their importance, particularly to figures associated with the Goddess of Sovereignty in her form as Maeb. In the story of Cu Chulainn, the Morrighan approaches him in various animal forms, one being a hornless red heifer, vexing him in battle. He breaks the heifer's leg, and later she appears as a milk-giving cow and allows him to drink from her three teats.

The Morrighan wanted to mate her bull Slemauir the Smooth with the cow owned by the "blameless woman" (some say man) Odras. Odras refuses. Morrighan lures the cow away through the woods and into a cave that leads to the otherworld. Odras follows. Morrighan then turns her uninvited guest into a pool of water. Some interpret this tale as Odras trying to cheat "death" and the cow had died and returned to the underworld of the land, and this is why she/he was punished. The cow is her wealth, her livelihood, and all that comes from the Earth must return to the Earth again.

In modern interpretations of shamanic totems, cow is the medicine of selfless giving, of unconditional love, nourishment and family. Hindu tradition reveres the cow for the same reasons. The bull in particular is associated with sacrifice. In many cultures, cattle and other large livestock are a symbol of wealth, and their magick is of prosperity and blessing in the financial world. All of these associations show many of the earthy associations of the Morrighan, rather than her sorcerous or warrior aspects.

Eel

The eel shows up a bit in Celtic legends and folklore. The Morrighan took on this form in one of her encounters with Cu Chulainn. His spear, Gae-Bolg, is associated with the eel's power, made from the bones of a sea monster. The eel is also a popular form in shapeshifting battle and duels. Its meaning in these tales is about defense and adaptability.

Eels are not the most popular totem in New Age lore, but what little is said about them in popular books gives them similar attributes in battle, through deception and disguise. By their nature, they are elusive. They are nocturnal and difficult to track. When not hunting, they hide, yet they are ambitious, hunting large prey with their strong and sharp teeth. They are the snakes of the sea. Some Neopagans see the snake itself, sacred to many goddess traditions, as a totem of the Morrighan. In Celtic lore, eels are said to come up on the land by growing feet when they want, so they are shapeshifters as well. They adapt to the given situation. The electric eel has also captured our fascination with its curious ability to generate voltage. Eels can have hidden and mysterious powers.

Wolf

Both the Morrighan and Badb are linked with the wolf. In her feud with Cu Chulainn, she prophecies that she will be "a grey wolf against thee....and I will strip a stripe of flesh from thee, from thy right hand till it extends to thy left." She later appears to Cu Chulainn as a female wolf, and distracts him in battle. He is able to throw her off and still defeat his opponent, but his foe, Loch, was able to wound him.

Wolves are strange figures in Celtic myth. Often seen as more predators than companions, they don't fit strongly into a lot of the myths we have. The story of Cu Chulainn is one of the few that does not involve Celtic Saints. When we look to the mythology of the world, we find that wolves are associated with their more positive attributes: protection, the skills of the warrior, loyalty to the pack and family. I learned to call upon the wolf totem for protection of self, family and home by my Witchcraft teachers. In some native American traditions, the wolf is the teacher of humanity, the keeper of sacred knowledge. They maintain complex, but balanced packs and humanity could learn a lot from them concerning the way we use our own resources and how we relate to each other. Wolf teaches us to be both grounded in family, and free; to be ritualistic, yet not bound by too much structure. We can be flexible and instinctive, intuitive. We can be wild, yet we can also be nourishing. Many stories associate wolves with humans, particularly stories of lycanthropy, transformation into wolf-man or woman. While we think of such ideas as the stuff of monster movies, they have their roots in the shamanic shapeshifting traditions. In Europe, the folk tales of werewolves were linked with vampires, faeries and Witches. They point to a deeper nature between humanity and our animalistic, totemic self. It is the part of the soul the Morrighan most often demonstrates in her stories.

Horse

The horse totem, while generally associated with the collective of the Morrighan, is usually the totem of Macha. Macha (and later Maeb) were believed to run faster than horses. This boast from Crunnchu, the husband of the fourth Macha, is what led her to the terrible race that resulted in the premature birth of her twins. To be able to do something like an animal suggests a shapeshifting connection. Macha uses the energy, the medicine, of the horse to race like a horse. Cu Chulainn's horse was called the "Grey of Macha" and wept blood the day he died. Twin colts are born on the same day Cu Chulainn is born. Perhaps they were another form of the twins of Macha?

Horse spirit is the embodiment of power. In mechanics, we even measure things in "horsepower." It's the ability to move, to get things done, to manifest. Obviously it's about movement and travel and the freedom that comes with travel. Horse teaches us to move in new directions, jump over obstacles and persevere to the end of the race, much like Macha. Due to the horse associations, Macha has been compared to Epona and Rhiannon, Celtic horse goddesses.

Totemic Beast Journey

This journey is done best with traditional core shamanic techniques. If you do not have someone in your life who can effectively drum for you, then use a recording. Ideally the drumming should be anywhere between 180-220 beats per minute (bpm), though some prefer as slow as 140 bpm, while others prefer closer to 300 bpm.

To attune culturally to the energy of the Morrighan, the use of a bodhran, an Irish drum with a double-headed beater, would be ideal. Though it is popular to attune to a shamanic trance state with a fast drum, culturally we have little evidence that the ancient Irish used drums. We do know they used bells, harps and various flutes and woodwinds. If you find recordings of Irish folk music, without words, but including instruments such as bells, harps, woodwinds and strings to be trance inducing and helpful to attune to the Morrighan and other Celtic deities, please use the music that is most helpful in achieving your magickal state.

Create a sacred space by casting a circle with the Four Fabled Cities, or if you prefer, create a sacred space more akin to the Celtic Reconstructionist Traditions and certain Traditional Craft practices, honoring the directions as they are recorded in myth and poem, not clockwise, but North to South, East to West, creating a crossroads. You can go to each direction with an offering, such as burning incense, or sprinkling water and salt.

To the North, to the land of Falias, the realm of the Stone and the guardians of this road.
To the South, to the land of Finias, the realm of the Spear and the guardians of this road.
To the East, to the land of Gorias, the realm of the Sword and the guardians of this road.
To the West, to the land of Murias, the realm of the Cup and the guardians of this road.
To the Sacred Center, to Tara, where all roads meet.
Beannacht! (Bahn-ukht)

I call to the Morrighan, to the Dark Lady.
I seek the wisdom of your animal incarnations.
I seek the wisdom of the beasts of flesh and blood.
I seek to know your ways through their magick, guidance and teaching.
I call upon the black-winged messengers, the Crow and Raven
Carrion feeders at the heart of the battlefield.
I call upon the four-legged ones, the Cow, the Horse and the Wolf.
I call upon your prosperity, your swiftness and your protection.
I call upon those who slither and crawl, the Eel and Serpent
Close to the ground, close to the Mother.
Share your blessings with me
And in return I share your blessing with the world.
Great Lady please aid me in this work
So mote it be.

Close your eyes. Breathe deeply. Relax yourself, starting at the top of your head and moving through your feet. Listen to the music you are using to effect your trance state.

In your mind's eye, envision a great tree in the center of the Emerald Isle. This is the world tree, the Shaman's or Witch's tree. This is the great oak of the Druids. It is the center of the world where all roads meet, and connects you to the Great Above of the Heavens and the Great Below of the deep Underworld. Only a thin veil, like gossamer, separates you from the tree. Step through the veil and stand before the tree. Feel its bark. Hear the wind in its branches. Smell the rich Earth where the roots dig deep.

Look into the roots for an opening, a tunnel. The roots could move to give you passage. The roots lead to a spiraling tunnel. The tunnel may rise up to the sky or down into the depths, or simply move between, deeper into the spirit world that is all around us.

Seek out the totems of the Morrighan. Seek the serpent and the eel. Seek the crow and raven. Seek the cow, the horse and the wolf. See who will come to be your teacher and guide in these journeys.

The animal spirit may commune with your verbally or nonverbally, depending on what will be best for you. It may beckon you to follow, teaching you by allowing you to observe its lessons in nature, preparing you for situations that will have both literal and symbolic meaning. Learn all you can from this ally and return often.

When done with your experience, return the way you came, through the tunnels of the world tree. Exit and thank the great tree for safe passage. Step back through the veil that separates you and let the tree image fade from your mind. Close your space.

I thank the Great Lady, the Morrighan, the Three in One.
I thank you, Lady of the Beasts, for granting me this blessing and lessons.
I thank the spirit of (name the animal you encountered) for our time together.
Blessed be.

To the North, to the land of Falias, the realm of the Stone, I thank you mighty guardians.
To the South, to the land of Finias, the realm of the Spear, I thank you mighty guardians.
To the East, to the land of Gorias, the realm of the Sword, I thank you mighty guardians.
To the West, to the land of Murias, the realm of the Cup, I thank you mighty guardians.
To the Sacred Center, to Tara, where all roads meet. I stand here always.
Beannacht! (Bahn-ukht)

Shapeshifting Journey

Shapeshifting means to take the shape of the animal ally, or truly, any other aspect of nature, in spirit vision and shamanic journey. The experience teaches you directly about the nature of that which you shift into. This is a common occurrence in core shamanic teachings, when the practitioner's self image in a journey either becomes the animal ally, or merges with an animal spirit. In the Celtic traditions, shapeshifting is a major part of myths and poems of the Druids and bards, and the shifts are not limited to animals, but features in the landscape, and even abstract concepts without physical form. This type of poetry shows up in the work attributed to the Welsh bard Taleisin, and particularly in the poem attributed to the Milesian Amergin, as his people invade Ireland in *The Song of Amergin*.

The Song of Amergin

I am a stag: of seven tines,
I am a flood: across a plain,
I am a wind: on a deep lake,
I am a tear: the Sun lets fall,
I am a hawk: above the cliff,
I am a thorn: beneath the nail,
I am a wonder: among flowers,
I am a wizard: who but I
Sets the cool head aflame with smoke?

I am a spear: that roars for blood,
I am a salmon: in a pool,
I am a lure: from paradise,
I am a hill: where poets walk,
I am a boar: ruthless and red,
I am a breaker: threatening doom,
I am a tide: that drags to death,
I am an infant: who but I
Peeps from the unhewn dolmen arch?

I am the womb: of every holt,
I am the blaze: on every hill,
I am the queen: of every hive,
I am the shield: for every head,
I am the tomb: of every hope.

(Translation by Robert Graves from *The White Goddess*)

A shapeshifting journey can occur through use of the same technique above in the Totemic Beast Journey, simply clarifying the intention is not just to journey with an animal spirit, but to shapeshift into one. Ideally you want to perform a shapeshifting exercise with an animal spirit with which you have already established a spiritual relationship, rather than a brand new one. For some practitioners, the experience is very visceral and even overpowering. Sensations of bones and muscles reshaping often occur. For others, it is more mental and abstract, but we cannot always predict which it will be prior to the experience.

Try this petition in place of the last, but otherwise keep with the form of the previous ritual.

I call to the Morrighan, to the Dark Lady.
I seek the wisdom of your animal incarnations.
I seek the wisdom of the beasts of flesh and blood.
I seek to be one with (name your animal ally).
Great Lady please aid me in this work,
For my Highest Good.
So mote it be.

A ritual posture that can facilitate the shape-shifting experience is known as The Machalilla Posture, based upon a ceramic urn found in Ecuador. While this sounds like nothing remotely associated with the Morrighan or Ireland, there is a reason for its inclusion. The practice of shamanically using postures found in ancient artifacts has been pioneered by the anthropologist Felicitas Goodman and her colleagues at the Cuyaungue Institute in Santa Fe, and popularized through the writings of her student Belinda Gore. The Machalilla posture is found in Gore's book *Ecstatic Body Postures*. The theory suggests that certain cultures had an intimate understanding of shamanic consciousness linked with body posture, and how certain postures facilitate certain types of journeys. These postures are like circuits, aiding us in attaining the type of journey we want, ranging from travel to divination to what is known as metamorphosis, which often means shapeshifting. While based upon American art, this metamorphosis posture is also reminiscent, if not exact, of a yoga position known as Crow, linking it in my experience to the Morrighan goddesses.

While in Hatha Yoga, Crow pose has the hands on the floor and the feet in the air like wings, which would not be particularly conducive to shamanic journey, the Kundalini Yoga Crow pose is more reminiscent of the Machalilla Posture. Kundalini Crow has the feet flat on the floor, legs shoulder width apart, knees bent, tail bone above the floor, toes pointing outwards, and arms reaching straight forward with index fingers pointing forward, like a beak, with other fingers interlaced. Back stays straight, gaze is over the extended arms and a rapid breath known as Breath of Fire is often performed with it. It is said to aid the clearing of the root chakra and eliminative system, grant strength to the legs and knees and balance the heart chakra.

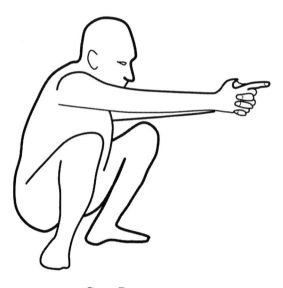

Crow Pose

A modified version can have you on the balls of your feet if feet flat on the floor is too difficult to maintain. A second modification has the hands resting on the knees, akin to the Machalilla Posture.

To hold the Machalilla Posture, you are actually sitting on the floor, unlike Crow. Gore instructs us:

"Sit on the floor with your legs as wide apart as possible, your knees bent and your legs drawn up toward your body. Your feet should be sole down on the floor. Arch your arms away from your body. With your right hand at your right knee and your left hand at your left knee, form the fingertips of each hand into a circle around their respective kneecap. It is as if you grasp each kneecap with your fingertips and gently tug on it. Rest your tongue between your lips as you face forward, your eyes closed."

— *Ecstatic Body Postures*, p. 153.

Practitioners emphasize that the tongue position is crucial to the success of this posture. The posture is very primal to me, reminiscent of the goddess giving birth.

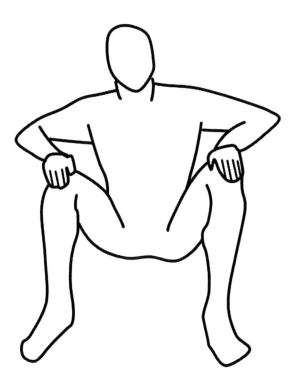

Machalilla Posture

For your shapeshifting journey with the Morrighan, experiment with either the Machalilla Posture or the Kundalini Crow pose to see if either facilitates the experience of metamorphosis and attunes you with the totems of the Morrighan.

OFFERINGS TO THE MORRIGHAN

While we typically think of totemic medicine exclusively in term of animal powers, technically anything has a healing power or magick, and medicine can even be more appropriately associated with plants and minerals. Plants, minerals, mountains, stars, anything at all can act in the role of a totem for those who see things through an animist's eyes, who see a world where everything has a vital and intelligent spirit. Everything, not just animals, can confer wisdom, power and love. Everything can guide and heal. The oldest forms of natural medicine used not only the spirits, but remedies made from animal parts, plants and minerals to effect healing physically and spiritually. While many today focus strictly on her warrior aspects, the Morrighan is said to be the "source of all enchantments, and appears to have "Witch-like" qualities to her character, so it would only be natural to assume she has knowledge of the use of magickal charms and herbs, even if there is no direct reference in the traditional Irish lore.

The gods of all cultures have had various substances, animal, vegetable and mineral, associated with them. Such substances would be used in temple offerings and rituals of devotion and sacrifice. They would be made into incense, oils and potions to attune one to the gods. Sadly, we don't have a lot of that information relating to the Celtic gods, as their myths have been recorded in such a late era compared to the classical writings of Greece, Rome, Egypt and India, from which we have a lot more information on statuary, offerings and herbs. Perhaps not being a temple tradition-oriented culture, the Celtic methods of devotion were different, as we don't have any evidence of a cult of the Morrighan as we do other ancient goddesses, but today's Pagan population seeks to reconnect with their gods in this way. Much of Neopaganism is a temple tradition, and even when working with the Celts or Norse, worship techniques more familiar to Egypt, Greece, Rome and Sumer creep into our practice. It's only natural. When the Romans invaded England, suddenly we gained statues and carvings of the Celts, where most likely the earlier Celtic traditions would never make permanent depictions of their gods. Through a process of reflection, communication and discovery, we have unearthed correspondences for the Morrighan.

One of the traditions of modern magick that has influenced Witchcraft and Neopaganism in general is the use of the Qabalah. While the Qabalah was originally a system of Jewish mysticism that was fused with Hermetic teachings and alchemy, the main visual symbol of the Qabalah, the Tree of Life, has become a versatile "map" where any structure from any religious tradition or system can be mapped onto its ten spheres and twenty-two lines. Each sphere, properly referred to as a sephira (plural sephiroth) refers to a dimension of consciousness and is associated with a planet, a deity archetype and a wide variety of stones, oils, herbs and other correspondences. By looking at the archetypal forces embodied by the Morrighan, along with color associations, we begin to gather some potential working correspondences for her. Most likely they were not associated with her in ancient Ireland, but our relationship with her evolves as the world grows smaller and more connected, so it's only natural that she'd find new things she would like. Tuning to the corresponding energetic vibration to deepen our love and understanding of an entity is a common occult practice.

By looking at her associations as a dark goddess of battle, death, sexuality and the land, we could easily associate the Morrighan with the sephira of Binah, Geburah, Netzach and Malkuth. These four sephiroth are associated with the planets Saturn, Mars, Venus and Earth respectively. Many would also include Yesod, the Moon, on that list. As much as I would like to do so, and in many of my goddess workings where the Morrighan was an aspect of the greater universal Goddess, the Moon and stars were a part of her body, but traditionally she is not a Moon goddess in the direct manner of Selene or Diana. Her associations with magick, sorcery and prophecy would be appropriate for Yesod, but there is no specific mention of the Moon in her lore. Strangely, there are few mythic mentions of the Moon in Celtic literature and no clear and true Moon goddess. The Morrighan is often cited as a dark Moon goddess, but that is a modern association. The Welsh Arianrhod could be considered lunar, but is also considered a star goddess due to her link with the starry castle. Author Sharynne MacLeod Nicmhacha explores the search for the Celtic Moon goddess in her excellent book, *Queen of the Night: The Celtic Moon Goddess in Our Lives.*

The Morrighan's most obvious associations are with Mars, as a goddess of battle and warriors and the carrion crow of the battlefield. We tend to think of the Martian energy as male in western occultism, but in Qabalah, the sephira of Gebura falls directly on the Pillar of Severity, usually considered negative and feminine. The pillar is topped with the sphere of Binah/Saturn, another planetary archetype often seen as male, but again in the Qabalah, it is portrayed as the dark goddess as the cosmic womb or void, from which all things usher forth. It is the mother for it is the first level of consciousness where things take form. Here we have the Morrighan in her most cosmic form, equated with Danu as the great mother of the gods and mother of all things.

Saturnine correspondences are usually black, toxic or earthy. Many of the toxic plants in the Witch's garden fall under the domain of Saturn. Myrrh is the traditional herb, along with patchouli, horsetail and comfrey, and the perfume is civet, the secretion from a civet cat, usually not used naturally in perfumery anymore due to animal rights concerns, though synthetics are available. Dark stones such as jet, onyx and obsidian are popular for Saturn as well. The star sapphire is Binah's gem as well.

In Geburah, we have the battle goddess, winnowing out the weak. The color of Mars is red, and all red and stimulating herbs are associated with it. Tobacco is the traditional scent, though many use the red resin of dragon's blood from a palm tree as a powerful correspondence to Mars. It adds power to anything, smells pleasing when burned and dispels all harmful forces. It's particularly good in exorcisms to remove all phantoms and astral garbage.

Netzach seems less likely for our goddess of battle, but in her guise as faery queen, Netzach would be her realm of enchantment. Its name translates to "Victory" but refers to the victory of love, not war. The fire of sexuality is a part of Netzach, as well as emotions, romance and the wild of nature. Venus's colors are green and pink. The incense is red sandalwood, the perfume is rose and all flowers associated with love and seduction fall under its influence. Many of the Witch's poisons are beautiful, like nightshade, belladonna, henbane and mandrake, and share rulership between Venus and Saturn.

Malkuth is the realm of planet Earth. It is embodied by the Goddess of the Land. Here we find the Morrighan as the Goddess of Sovereignty. She is the material world, and in the traditional lore, Ireland. The colors of Malkuth are traditionally black, red (russet), green (olivine), and yellow (citrine). The incense is Dittany of Crete, for its ability to give a body of smoke to astral entities, though Patchouli is sometimes used instead, showing the link between Saturn and the Earth.

Modern practitioners tend to favor the following correspondences when working with the Morrighan in devotion or magick:

Herbs	**Trees**	**Stones**
Dragon's Blood	Blackthorn	Obsidian
Patchouli	Willow	Ruby
Myrrh	Elder	Garnet
Ambrette Seed	Yew	Onyx
Mugwort		Jet
Wormwood		
Nightshade		
Henbane		
Cinnamon		
Rose		
Vervain		

While many of the herbs of modern Morrighan association have little to do with anything native to Ireland, it is possible to work with herbs that are native to, or are currently growing well in Ireland today. If we look at the Morrighan as the Goddess of Irish sovereignty, anything growing upon the body of Ériu would be a potential herb for her worship and magick. Some seem more in harmony with her obvious natures than others, but the following plants, found in Ireland, can be used in Morrighan magick and offerings. I've purposely kept some of the species vague, as most of us are not living in Ireland, so we might not be able to get a specific native Irish variety, but our own local plants can resonate with a similar spiritual note as the native Irish.

Aconite	Caraway	Enchanter's Nightshade
Adder's Tongue	Celery	Eyebright
Agrimony	Chickweed	Fern
Alder	Chive	Foxglove
Angelica	Clubmoss	Fumitory
Betony	Comfrey	Garlic
Black Currant	Cotton Grass	Gorse
Blackthorn	Cornflower	Hawthorn
Broom	Cowslip	Heather
Burdock	Dandelion	Hemlock
Buttercup	Elecampane	Honesty

Horsetail	Onion	Strawberry
Iris, Yellow	Orchid	St. John's Wort
Ivy	Pansy	Summer Snowflake
Lady's Mantle	Pennyroyal	Sweet Cicely
Leek	Peppermint	Tansy
Loosestrife, Purple	Periwinkle, Lesser	Turnip
Marsh Marigold	Poppy	Vetch
Masterwort	Primrose	Violet
Mistletoe	Raspberry	White Bryony
Moonwort	Red Clover	Wild Oat
Mugwort	Rose of Sharon	Woodruff
Mullein	Shepherd's Purse	Yarrow
Mustard	Snapdragon	
Nettle	Spearmint	

The most famous Wiccan Morrighan incense comes from Janet and Stewart Farrar, from their book, *The Witch's Goddess*. Their formula includes musk ambrette, dragon's blood, patchouli essential oil, civet oil and four drops of blood from your own finger, to be mixed on the dark Moon, sealed in a jar and buried in the Earth for four weeks before using.

The Cabot Tradition of Witchcraft often honors Macha, particularly around Samhain and Lughnasadh, and uses several simple oils and powders at those celebrations. In more traditional occult lore, a dram is twenty drops, as is the measure used by Laurie Cabot. These recipes and rituals can be found in Laurie's book, *Celebrate the Earth*.

Macha Oil (No. 1)

   2 drams of grapeseed oil
   1 dram of Hemlock oil
   1 dram of Pine oil
   2 dried Mushrooms
   1 crow Feather

Macha Oil (No. 2)

   1 dram Grapeseed Oil
   1 dram Corn Oil

1 Piece of Obsidian

1 piece of crow feather

Macha Philter

Pine Needles

Mushrooms

Rosemary

Sunflower Petals

Sage

Apple Leaves

The Cabot Tradition also uses the very obvious correspondence of black feathers, particularly crows and ravens, in a method of seeking justice for terrible wrongs that have been done. This working does not hold a specific intention other than justice, and invokes the power of Macha specifically for the unjust way she was treated while pregnant. Black feathers are given to or sent to the perpetrator in Macha's name until the wrong is exposed and justice is done.

Black feathers can also obviously be used in other ways to align with the magick of the Morrighan and her dark-winged totems. They can decorate altars, be used in potions and made into smudge fans. It is important to know that in many places, including the U.S., it is illegal to own crow and raven feathers, even if they are found, without special dispensation. Many will use black dyed chicken feathers as a substitute.

Below are some of my own formulas for working with the Morrighan.

Morrighan Incense

3 Parts Red Sandalwood

1 Part Dragon's Blood

1 Part Cinnamon

1/2 Part Myrrh

1/2 Part Patchouli

1/2 Part Mugwort

1/2 Part Wormwood

1/2 Part Caraway Seed

1/4 Part Hawthorne Berry

1/4 Part Lady's Mantle

1/4 Part Red Raspberry Leaf

1/4 Part Rose Petals

9 drops Ambrette Essential Oil

3 drops Myrrh Essential Oil

3 drops Patchouli Essential Oil

3 drops Rose Essential Oil

Red Wine

Honey

A general all purpose incense to be used in any Morrighan working or offering.

Morrighan Oil

1 oz Crushed Dragon's Blood in Almond Oil

7 drops of Ambrette Seed Essential Oil

3 drops of Patchouli Essential Oil

3 drops of Rosewood Essential Oil

2 drops of Myrrh Essential Oil

1 drop of Cinnamon Bark Essential Oil

Wear three drops on the wrist or third eye to attune to the Morrighan.

Morrighan Prophecy Incense

2 Parts Dragon's Blood

2 Parts Mugwort

1 Part Myrrh

1 Part Wormwood

1/2 Part Eyebright

1/2 Part Poppy Seed

1/2 Part Angelica Root

1/2 Part Yarrow

1 Pinch Mistletoe

Red Wine

Honey

Burn when doing prophetic workings seeking answers and insights.

Morrighan Elixir

Alcohol (80 proof or higher vodka)

Red Raspberries

Apple Slices

Nettle Leaf

Vervain

Drink in devotional rituals. Also the elixir is a wonderful aid in the shapeshifting rite in this chapter.

Warrior Queen Incense

3 Parts Tobacco (Natural)

1 Part Red Sandalwood

1 part Myrrh

1 Part Dragon's Blood

1/2 Part Patchouli

5 Drops of Myrrh Oil

4 Drops of Patchouli Oil

5 Parts Whiskey

Burn for victory and success in your battles. Write your intentions for success out on paper in red ink and waft the paper through this smoke before you burn your petition.

Phantom Queen (Burn Outside, Well Ventilated)

3 Parts Mugwort

2 Parts Wormwood

2 Parts Myrrh

1 Part Mullein Leaf

1 Part Vervain

1/2 Part Yew Needles

1/2 Part Henbane Leaf

1/4 Part Datura Seeds

1/4 Part Garlic

9 Parts Brandy

Burn to work with the spirits of the ancestors, the dead or to communicate with and clear unwanted ghosts and spirits. A great incense for working with the Morrighan on Samhain.

Morgana the Faery Queen Incense

1 Part Lavender

1 Part Sandalwood

1 Part Orris Root

1 Part Willow Bark

1/2 Part Yarrow

1/2 Part Elecampane

1/2 Part Rose Petals

1/4 Part Hawthorn Berry

1/4 Part Elder Berry

10 Drops Lavender Oil

5 Drops Rosewood Oil

1 Part Honey

Burn to attune to the Faery aspect of the Morrighan and her guise as Morgan of Avalon.

Faery Queen Oil

7 Drops Lavender Oil

5 Drops Sandalwood Oil

1 Drop Yarrow Oil

3 Drops Rose Oil (Substitute Rosewood if necessary)

1 Dried Elder Berry Whole

Anoint your third eye to commune with and see faery beings.

Morrighan Devotional Incense

1 Part Pine Needle

1 Part Willow Bark

1 Part Vervain

1 Part Tobacco

1 Part Red Clover

Burn as a simple offering to the Morrighan in any of her guises.

Danu Incense

3 Parts Sandalwood

1 Part Angelica Root

1 Part Mugwort

1 Part Heather

1 Part Peppermint

1/2 Part Lady's Mantle

1/2 Part Nettle

1/2 Part Dandelion Root

1/2 Part Horsetail

1 Part Honey

Burn to attune to the Great Mother. An earthy scent that burns quickly. Add perfumes and more pleasant smelling resins if you want something fancier, though these herbs chosen encompass a wide range of correspondences for the cosmic manifestation of the Mother Danu.

For all the incenses, the alcohol, honey and oils are used to bind. Mix the dry powdered ingredients thoroughly and then add the wet ingredients, again mixing well. Let them dry without exposure to heat and light. The mass can be broken into smaller pieces ideal to burn on charcoal diskettes found in any occult supply shop.

You can also use the incense as a magickal powder, carrying it as a charm, or placing it in a bag along with a stone or crystal, wood, or other charm to evoke the Morrighan's aid in a particular spell or intention. The oils can be used to anoint not only the self, but ritual tools and power objects dedicated to the goddess.

Other offerings on a Morrighan altar or in a ritual devoted to the great Queen would be anything having to do with death, including death fetishes of skulls and skeletons. Many Mexican traditions make sugar skulls in honor of the Day of the Dead. Anything with warrior imagery would also be appropriate. Historically appropriate, but less appealing to modern Pagans, are offerings of meat and carrion, for many of her totems are meat and carrion feeders. With the cow associations, a spiced or flavored milk or homemade dairy products could work as offering, libation and sacrament. I also find alcohol, particularly Irish Whiskey, is favored.

Lady of the Isle

Green by Day
Black by Night
I offer this smoke to you.
By the four Sacred Cities
And the secret fifth within your heart.
Hear my works.
Know my truth.
Feel my love.
Lady of the Battle
White by Day
Black by Night
Walk with me on the gameboard of life.
Watch my words.
Guide my way.
Guard my back.
Lady of the Phantoms
Red by Day
Black by Night
Lead me when my time comes.
Flow in my blood.
Breathe in my breath.
Be in my bones.
Now and to the end of time.
So mote it be.

Chapter Six
Mistress of Battle

The most striking image of the Morrighan is the warrior, though strangely, most manifestations of the goddess do not take up arms and use weapons, though she is associated with many figures who do. While a goddess of battle, she is best known for inciting battle, and her interactions with figures such as Lugh and Cu Cuhulainn spur them into battle. Her vexing nature, even to those who at first appear to be allies, is considered either punishment for disrespect to the goddess, or spiritual warrior training. They are battles that make the soul stronger for the final outcome. Even though she is considered a master of battle, often those allied with her do not have complete success on the battlefield. In that way, the battlefield is much like life, and from the perspective of this goddess, dying is not always losing, but returning to her embrace.

Battle is a metaphor for life. Many of the Indo-European traditions are what we would consider warrior cultures, and the road of the warrior is just as much a path to enlightenment as the mystic's path. In some traditions, the two are not so easily divided, even though many of us have an overly sentimentalized idea of spirituality as equated with pacifism. In the Toltec traditions, a shaman-sorcerer is considered a warrior. Many of the yogic traditions, seemingly peaceful, are very martial in nature, and the mental stance is one of a spiritual warrior. The enemies are the forces within that would oppose your enlightenment, not outside contenders, but you are a warrior nonetheless. The sacred Hindu text of the Bahgava Gita is based on the notion of the warrior, Arjuna, doing his "duty" in battle. Buddhist Shamballa traditions look to the peaceful warrior, as do the Sihks. Native American traditions honor the warrior. The virtues of the heathen traditions are exemplified by a warrior.

The Morrighan's teachings, at their heart, are no different. They teach us about the adversity of life, from seemingly outside forces to the forces within. All the figures of Celtic mythology can be seen as quasi-historic in a folkloric tradition, or mythic, symbolizing larger shifts in the history of not just Ireland, but all the world. Are the Fomorians a memory of an earlier stone age race, or the embodiment of a pre-human age of chaos akin to the Titans of Greek myth? Depends on who you ask. But the teachings of the Tuatha's battles with them, and the role of the Morrighan in those battles, teaches us many of the same lessons of being in alignment with the goddess regardless of the interpretation you choose. At the heart of the warrior's lessons, from the earliest invasion of Ireland to the myths of King Arthur, is the notion of how the warrior serves the goddess, serves the land and lives in right accord. Those that do not are destined to failure. It's a lesson our modern day warriors, and Pagans, need to learn. Perhaps not all will see their service to the goddess, but service to a higher force, a higher principle is the true way of the warrior.

The Morrighan's role as a battle goddess can be, fittingly, divided into three main functions. She uses sorcery and magick to fight. She takes direct action as a warrior. And she trains, tutors and most importantly, challenges the warrior to rise up.

THE SORCEROUS BATTLES

While we might think of battle only coming in the form of sword and spear to flesh when we think of the Celts, the earliest episodes of battle involving the Morrighan depict scenes where she, and other Witch women, increase the odds for the Tuatha de Dannan using magick upon the battlefield. While we depict modern images of the Morrighan and her associated goddesses as warriors, with swords, shields and spears, she is most often on the sidelines of the battlefield, provoking war, and as the carrion crow, taking her spoils of the dead. Her magick is the way she involves herself in battle.

In the Tuatha's first war, the war with the Fir Bolgs, Morrigan, Badb and Macha cast a spell together over the battlefield. The three goddesses bring down "enchanted showers of might," "mighty showers of fire," and a "downpour of red blood." These showers prevent the enemies from moving for three days and three nights. This gives quite a tactical advantage, assuming it only affected the Fir Bolgs.

The motives of the three sorceresses are not always clear. They boast among the gods, along with Danu, in one of her rare incarnate appearances. They will fight too, but upon the battlefield, the three plus Danu and Be Chuille, their "foster mothers," also cast a spell fixing "stone pillars" to mark the line of the battlefield, with a magickal charm preventing the warriors from fleeing past the markers until the stones themselves flee. Retreat was not allowed, presumably for either side, but the effort appears for the Tuatha in this case.

In the aspect of Nemain, her cries and shriek can not only confuse and cause fear, but also magickally cause the death of her enemies, while rallying the blood of her allies. While amongst the Tuatha, the Morrighan boasts she shall destroy whatever she has her eye on, implying a supernatural power to destroy, not just a tenacity. The eyes are conduits of magick, and the world over the eye is associated with malefic magick, as in the case of the classic evil eye. The gaze of a fixed eye can bewitch, fascinate or destroy when applied properly.

One could also consider her various shapeshifting episodes into animals that torment and attack Cu Cuhulainn as a form of sorcerous attack. Stories ranging from folklore, like the tale of *The Twa Magicians,* to popular fantasy, such as Neil Gaimen's *The Sandman: Preludes and Nocturnes,* have stories of magickal creatures dueling it out through shapeshifting. Whoever is more powerful, or even better, more clever, can win the battle. It's a contest of power, wits and magick. While her opponent does not shift his shape, perhaps if he were a better student and did, the tale would have ended differently and new magick would have been learned.

WARRIOR WOMAN

Despite our view of Morrighan as a warrior, there are very few references to her in the lore taking direct action as a warrior. One of the few direct attacks made by the Morrighan is in the Second Battle of Moytura, and it is confused at best. She tells the Dagda that she will kill the Fomorian leader Indech, allied with Balor. She says she will take his heart's blood and testicles, and use it to anoint and bless the Tuatha warriors with his power. Either she kills him directly as a declaration of her loyalty to the Tuatha's cause, or she magickally drains him of his blood and "manhood" while he is later killed by Oghma. In either case, she appears to be performing the role of a priestess, blessing and anointing the warriors for future battle, taking life from one and granting it to another.

The most striking warrior queen figure directly tied to the Morrighan is Macha Mongruad. She acts as warrior and queen to keep her throne, and while a skilled hunter and tracker, to track down the sons of Dithorba she uses cunning and subtlety, rather than brute force and violence to rule the day. In some ways, this Macha, and in fact, all the Morrighan figures, can be considered to be akin to Athena of the Greeks, a battle goddess who uses strategy rather than force whenever possible. But the lack of force should not be taken as a sign of weakness or ineptitude, rather a wisdom to win by the most effective means necessary.

Other warrior figures include Queen Mebd, as discussed with the goddesses of the five provinces and then Scathach, who, as tutor to Cu Cuhulainn, could be seen as an aspect of the Morrighan.

TEACHER AND TUTOR

The teacher and tutor function of the Morrighan is not always obvious. Many times she appears to be as much of a trouble maker and antagonist, if not outright enemy of the hero, but that is in many ways how she functions. Like a harsh taskmaster, she pulls no punches. She speaks and shows what others would fear to point out, but what is necessary to reach the next level. Her testing can make you stronger. The forces she sets in motion are for the next stage of evolution. While seemingly personal, nothing of what she does is motivated by personal interest, but for the balance of the land and cosmos.

Like the interplay of Goddess and God, of priestess and priest or simply of lovers, she seems to both encourage and antagonize the strong male figures of the story. In truth, their power, as Sovereignty, flows from her, but that is not always clear in the telling of the tale. Perhaps it is not always clear to the god, king or hero in question. It appears the earlier gods of the Tuatha are on slightly better terms with her, but by the time Lugh's "avatar" is on the scene, in the form of Cu Cuhulainn, some of the old ways are being forgotten, and the Goddess is disrespected. Perhaps this is a foreshadowing of things to come, and her terrible prophecy for the end of the world at the end of the Second Battle of Moytura.

In the battle with the Fomorians, Morrighan instigates the battle, urging Lugh to take action, a "battle of overthrowing." She is the impetus of the battle, and she chooses her champion, the god of lightning and light and many skills, to be her hand in the world. His light is a balance to her darkness. His direct action counterpoints her shadowy working behind the scenes, yet the two make an effective pair.

Also in the Second Battle, she advises the Dagda as they come together on the Ford of Unshin. Unlike Lugh, the Dagda seems to be on equal stature with the goddess as a titanic force. The two make love at the ford, and she offers her power and strategy to the Tuatha. She is tutor in the sense of acting like counselor and advisor, and even blesses the warriors with the blood of their enemies.

The student she is most famous for tutoring though, in the most difficult ways, is the hero Cu Cuhulainn. He is considered an aspect of Lugh reborn, described by some as Lugh's avatar, just as the Hindu deities incarnate in earthly bodies in each age. Their relationship has been compared to the Sumerian figures of Inanna and Gilgamesh. At times they appear like foes, yet they are really in a complex tutelary relationship of goddess and priest-warrior. Though lacking the romantic aspect, one could look at the relationship between Hera and Hercules much the same way. She provides directly and indirectly twelve labors to perform, and pretty much torments him for much of his life, but in the end, she is a higher force that eventually brings about his ascent to Olympus. It's easy in our modern age of black and white, good and bad characters in a story to miss these complex relationships of an earlier time, but if you dig deep, including into the story of Cu Cuhulainn, you will find it. They are good reminders for us all when we get into a tutoring relationship with a matron goddess, that such figures will not be all sweetness and light, particularly when the Morrighan chooses you. Be careful of the gods you accept into your life.

Cu Cuhulainn was born when the men of Ulster, including King Conchobar mac Nessa and his daughter Deichtine, go hunting a magickal flock of birds. Though never specifically cited as crows or ravens, one has to wonder with the child's later connection to the Morrighan. They find shelter from the snow with a host where the wife of the family is pregnant with child, and then goes into labor. Deichtine helps her with her labor. At the same time, a mare births twin colts. At dawn, the Ulster men find that the house is gone, and they have been transported to the Neolithic mount in New Grange, but the child and twin horses are still with them. While Deichtine mothers the child, the child grows very ill and dies. The god Lugh appears to her and reveals he was the host of the Ulster men that night, and puts the child in her womb to give rebirth to. Lugh names the child Setanta. There is great scandal over the pregnancy, but eventually she has a child named Setanta.

The boy has an unusual childhood, culminating in his encounter with Culann's hounds. Culann invites Conchobar to a feast, and Conchobar invites Setanta, who is playing a game of hurling with the other boys. He arrives later, after Culann has released his massive dogs to protect his estate. They attack Setanta, who unexpectedly kills one to defend himself. Culann is distraught and Setanta agrees to replace the hound, and until he can, he will guard the house like Culann's hound, earning his name Cu Cuhulainn, meaning "Culann's hound," from the Druid Cathbad who was in attendance at the feast.

While still a boy, Cu Cuhulainn encounters Badb. First he encounters a specter carrying a corpse, who tells Cu Cuhulainn to carry it. He refuses and the two, Cu Cuhulainn and phantom, fight. Badb appears and mocks Cu Cuhulainn, who gets so angry, he beheads the phantom and plays with the head like a ball. He goes on to find and rescue the king and the king's missing son on the battlefield. Badb spurred him to action using insult, which sounds strange, but is the action of a harsh teacher, using ridicule and shame to motivate. Such methods are common amongst the Celts. As the Phantom Queen, did she send this specter to him on purpose?

Later Cu Cuhulainn encounters Scathach the warrior woman for training. While not specifically the Morrighan, many see Scathach as another manifestation of the Morrighan as a teacher. Her daughter Uathach reveals to Cu Cuhulainn that he must make three demands of her mother: teaching without neglect, prophecy of his future and marriage to Uathach without wedding gifts. She agrees to all three. On the day he takes weapons at Emain Macha, it is prophesized the warrior would be famous, but his life would be short.

During the Cattle Raid of Cooley, he has direct confrontation with the Morrigan proper. Just before combat, a royal woman approaches Cu Cuhulainn, wanting to make love to him, and he refuses. In truth, she is the Morrighan, and vows to have vengeance upon him for this insult. In another version of their first meeting, she appears as a charioteer, with the otherworldly horse and chariot, and a silent man with a cow in tow. Cu Cuhulainn believes it to be the cow of Ulster, which he is bound to protect, and questions the man. He is silent, but the woman responds, mocking him. Only after she mysteriously disappears, setting events in motion, does he realize that she was the Morrighan. She leaves behind a crow, and the crow says, "I am guarding your death and I will continue to guard it." Is that a promise of protection, or a threat of death? In either case, in his first encounter he is brash and disrespectful, leading to his conflict with the Morrighan.

She attacks him, but not as herself. She attacks in the forms of animals, as if nature itself has risen up against him during his battle, testing him. She takes the form of an eel, tripping him in the waters of the ford. Cu Cuhulainn fights back and smashes her ribs. Next she becomes a wolf and causes a cattle stampede, yet she loses an eye to Cu Cuhulainn due to his skilled shot with a sling. Her last incarnation of attack is strangely of a heifer, leading the stampede, but he manages to break her leg, again using a sling.

While not quite the same, this portion of the tale is reminiscent of the Welsh magician Gwydion's "training" and punishment, being transformed into a stag, sow and wolf, each for a year as punishment for his aiding his brother Gilaethwy in the rape of Goewin. Gilaethwy was transformed into the animals' mates, and they reproduced, creating three offspring, one of each species. Each animal is seen today by many Witches as a symbolic initiatory rank of a deeper mystery, rather than as simple punishment. While the mysteries of the Stag/Deer, Boar/Sow and Wolf/She-Wolf can confer much wisdom, they can make us wonder about the mysteries of the eel, wolf, and cow in the context of the Morrighan as warrior-teacher.

After his victory, she appears as a crone with a cow, milking the beast before Cu Cuhulainn. This fairy cow has only three teats, another indication this is not a normal encounter, as three is the Morrighan's sacred number. The crone has broken ribs, a broken leg, and a missing eye. It appears that, despite the clues, the crone still tricked Cu Cuhulainn. She offers him milk, three drinks, and with each, he offers a blessing, healing each of her wounds. This shows both reciprocity between the hero and goddess, and that, as the son of Lugh, his power has grown to be on somewhat of an equal footing with the gods and other major Celtic powers, for he has the ability to both injure and heal such a goddess. The battles and testing, while seemingly from an insult, really further his ascent into greater power.

Later, he encounters Nemain, a form of the Morrighan that actually helps him. Her shrieks killed a hundred warriors in the opposing army of Queen Medb. Does this indicate that there is forgiveness and aid for Cu Cuhulainn? Perhaps the exchange with the cow has healed the rift between goddess and demigod-avatar.

In fact, his power only wanes when he breaks his geasa, or particular taboos. A geis is a religious restriction placed upon those of power, and when they are broken, power and respect is lost. Cu Cuhulainn has two in particular. He cannot refuse hospitality, which is a prominent taboo throughout the Celtic lands and plays a role in many stories, and he cannot eat the meat of his namesake, the dog or hound. When a crone offers him dog meat prepared as a meal, he either breaks one geis or the other. He was offered the meal by a crone, so many believe it was a guise of the Morrighan, giving him his final test. If there was a "right" choice, I'm not sure what it was. Perhaps the final lesson was the paradox of the choice and the inevitability of death, and this goddess ultimately held the power of life and death over him, even for a hero who seemingly had power over her.

In his final battle with Lugaid, three magickal spears are used against him, prophesized to kill three kings, one each. The first spear kills Cu Cuhulainn's charioteer, considered the king of charioteers. The second spear kills Liath Macha, Cu Cuhulainn's horse, considered the king of horses. The third and final spear mortally wounds Cu Cuhulainn, disemboweling him. He props himself up against a standing stone and ties himself there, to die on his feet, not on the ground and will not relinquish life. A crow lands on his shoulders, signaling to his enemies he is dead. Even as they behead him, he is engulfed in the light of heroes and deities, and his falling sword severs Ligaid's hand. Cu Cuhulainn's severed head is later placed upon a mast in the meadow where the Ulster men defeat the armies of Lugaid.

You can also see parallels between the more modern versions of the Arthurian mythos with Morgan Le Fey and King Arthur. Originally, she was simply one of nine sisters on the fabled isle, but in later renderings of the Camelot tale, she becomes his half-sister and adversary. Though usually depicted as spiteful and scheming, when looked at from the vantage point of divine will, she is a terrible dark goddess, testing the hero, making sure he is worthy of his role as King of the land. Her testing makes him stronger, although ultimately he appears to fail. Ultimately she is his teacher through the initiations of life and his many battles. Some cite twelve or thirteen battles of Arthur, much like Hercules through his twelve zodiac labors. It's only in the most modern lore that she is fully restored to that of a healer, and her negative actions can be more clearly seen from the view of a higher will at work through this priestess of Avalon.

In these tales she is not one sister out of nine, but usually one of three or four, with Elaine and Morgause most popularly linked to her. Her stories include arranging the theft of the scabbard of Excalibur, which is not only a goddess symbol like the grail, but it prevents the owner from bleeding to death. Without it, Arthur is vulnerable. She also sends a magickal cup or horn to the court of the Round Table, from which no unfaithful woman can drink without spilling the contents of the cup. In this plan, she hoped to reveal Guinevere and Lancelot's infidelity to the King and perhaps to the land. Morgan's attacks are not direct, like the animal attacks of the Morrighan, but serve the same purpose, testing and ultimately weakening the hero.

Arthur is drawn back to the land, or to the island, upon his failure, and she is there waiting for him, guiding his journey. Like the Morrighan, there appears to be forgiveness or at least understanding at the end of the journey.

The Lorica of the Morrighan

Lorica loosely translates to "breastplate," and Lorica prayers are those that "armor" you in divine protection. While they are often assumed to be Christian in origin, as the Lorica of St. Patrick is the most famous, in truth, these types of prayers and invocations date back to Sumeria, and patterns similar to the Sumerian prayers can be found in modern ceremonial magick, within the angelic invocation of the Lesser Banishing Ritual of the Pentagram. This particular Lorica, rather than invoke the power of Christ and the Christian god as St. Patrick does, calls upon the blessings of the Morrighan.

Today I rise upon the green Earth
Through the blessings of the Morrighan
Three in one and one in Three
Anu, Badb Catha and Macha Nemain
Forever a mystery.

Today I rise up
By the call of the Phantom Queen
By the love of the Faery Queen
By the strength of the Warrior Queen
By the wisdom of the Earthly Queen
By the magick of Sovereignty
I answer your call.

Today I rise up
And take my fate with you
Today I rise up
And seek my own vision of the future
Today I rise up
And walk upon the battlefield of life
Ready with you by my side, behind me and before me.

By the Love of the Dagda
Love me.
By the Path of the Warrior

Teach me.
By the Magick of the Sorceress
Enchant me.

Teacher of Cu Cuhulainn
Lover of the Dagda
Sisters to Ériu, Banba and Fódla
Daughter of Ernmas
Goddess of the Nine Waves of Creation
Bless me.

Bless me with your love, strength and wisdom.
Bless me with your courage, counsel and protection.
Bless me with your vision, power and fury.
Bless me.

By the blessings of Badb the battle crow
May I be prepared for what life has to offer me.
By the blessings of Macha in the sacred field,
May I always know my home and swiftly find my roots.
By the blessings of Nemain of the fierce battle cry
May I always speak my voice and know my truth.
Bless me.

May the powers of the dark-winged crow fly with me.
May I keep the sacred law.
May the whispers of the raven's song be with me,
Opening the gate to the Mysteries.
May the speed of the horse be in my steps,
Guiding me on the path.
May the gifts of the cow be given,
Nourishing me on my way
May the howl of the wolves run with me,
Leading me to my pack.

May the slitherings of the serpent upon land and water
Draw me back to the Great Mother.

Morrighan of the Bramble Thorn
Morrighan of the Ripest Berry
May I respect both your ways.
Call the phantoms to guide and protect me
In the realms of Earth and Spirit.
Call the faeries to watch and welcome me
In the enchanted lands beyond
Call the gods themselves to invite me to their table
In the halls of Tara with the eternal flame.

Today I rise up
Protect me from the North, from the land of Falias.
Guide me in the way of the Stone that cries out for the king.
Protect me from the South, from the land of Finias.
Guide me in the way of the Spear of Victory flashing like lightning
Protect me from the East, from the land of Gorias.
Guide me in the way of the Sword that shows only truth.
Protect me from the West, from the land of Murias
Guide me in the way of the ever plenty cauldron-cup.
Protect my heart. Protect my head. Protect my body.
Protect my Soul and Spirit Eternal.
Protect the blood of my ancestors
And the Cauldron of Inspiration
So I shall ever reside in the center, Meath, in Tara Eternal.

Beannacht! (Bahn-ukht)

Recite this as a morning prayer or whenever you feel the call of the Morrighan is needed for guidance, blessing and protection.

CHAPTER SEVEN
Children, Lovers and Husbands

Who are those closest to us? Children and lovers. In astrology, they are ruled by the Fifth House, which is where our ego is built up and taken down again. In many ways, that has been the role of our goddess, to build us up to work in the world, but to dismantle those things within us that no longer serve and eventually to bring us home. We become strong, but not too strong, or too proud and ego driven, to understand our work is done in the name of Sovereignty, the Goddess of the Land.

For a goddess of sexuality and fertility, we expect her stories to have many children, lovers and husbands. Yet in some ways, the tales of the Morrighan are tame in comparison with the trysts and offspring of the Greek and Roman pantheon. This makes her family even more important to look at, as they are not indiscriminate. Each family member reveals an aspect of the dark lady. Through understanding these connections, we can further understand her.

CHILDREN OF THE GODDESS

The Morrighan proper, despite being a goddess of sexuality and fertility, doesn't have much in the way of descendants. According to *The Book of Invasions*, the Morrigu, also known as Anand, is said to have three sons: Glon, Gaim, and Coscar, though about them little is known other than their names.

One of the Morrighan's more mysterious sons is Meich. According to Phillip Gardiner in *Gateways to the Otherworld,* this son of the Morrighan had three hearts, and each one contained a serpent. Gardiner notes the image was used in alchemy and to followers of this goddess, points to a poisonous or toxic nature she can have, like the eels or serpents she can become. But it also shows the triple nature of the self, of the heart, one for each of her three manifestations. In his book *Secret Societies: Gardiner's Forbidden Knowledge,* he makes comparisons to an area in Avebury and a heart formation of stone and the serpentine associations with stone circles such as Avebury with the snake and heart myth of Meich. Though I love the image of the Morrighan's son having three hearts with serpents, I have to admit I can find no classical reference to this myth in the traditional Irish literature.

While Badb and Nemain both appear with no references to children, Macha on the other hand is the goddess of fertility in terms of children. Macha's, wife of Crunnchu, whole story revolves around her pregnancy and giving birth to twins upon the finish line at the race she is forced to run. But what happens to those children? We never really find out. It is assumed that they either die or are taken by their mother back to the faery realm. Hints are given about the twin horses that are born on the same night as Cu Cuhulainn.

Two horses are born the night of Cu Cuhulainn's birth, named Liath Macha, or Grey of Macha, and Dub Sainglend, Black of Saingliu. While seemingly wild faery horses, they cannot throw off Cu Cuhulainn, and are tamed by him to be his chariot horses. On the day of his death, Liath Macha refuses to allow Cu Cuhulainn's charioteer to harness him. Liath Macha only agrees when Cu Cuhulainn comes to harness him, but the gray horse weeps blood on that day. He is hit by a spear from Laeg. While the "King of Horses" is seemingly killed, he goes on to protect Dub Sainglend, by killing enemy warriors with his hooves and teeth. Dub Sainglend leads their allies to Cu Cuhulainn's body, and eventually returns to a pool in Linn Liaith, returning back to the faery realm.

They are never explicitly stated as the children of Macha, and in fact, might have nothing to do with them, but they are the only other reference of living twins associated with Macha.

While Ugaine Mor is the actual son of two different parents, he is considered a child of Macha as he was the foster son of Macha Mong Ruad and Cimbaeth. He avenged his foster mother's death by slaying her killer who sat upon the throne, Rechtaid Riderg, and then ascended to the throne of the High King of Ireland. His rule was legendary, even for a High King. Stories say he ruled not only Ireland, but all of Britain and possibly much of Europe. While mythic hyperbole, it does tell us the status of his kingship. Ugaine married a Gaulish princess and together they had twenty-two sons and three daughters. The number of children, siblings and servants a mythic figure has often points to a divine power. The twenty-two sons is reminiscent of the Major Arcana and letters of the Hebrew alphabet, even though they play no role in ancient Irish myth. The three daughters are another manifestation of the triple goddess, like the Morrighan herself. Before the division of the five provinces, he divided Ireland into twenty-five parcels, for all of his children. Ugaine Mor ruled Ireland until he was assassinated by Bodbchad, his brother, who lasted a whole day and half upon the throne before being killed by Ugaine's son, Loegraire.

The Arthurian tales gives us a little more Greco-Roman drama of lovers, children and bastard offspring. Once the figure of Morgana Le Fey is taken off the island and transformed into a more human sorceress, she is usually depicted as the unhappy wife of Urien, King of Gore. Her son is Ywain.

Ywain, or Owain in Welsh mythology, makes an interesting connection for Morgan to other primal goddess figures. Owain is the son of Modron in Welsh myth, the primal mother, equivalent to Danu to the Irish. Morgan is listed as his mother in the French tales of Camelot, though initially they are not listed as mother and son in their first tales. But later the link is clear with Ywain the son of Urien. Ywain was based upon a historic figure, and soon became wrapped into the Arthurian myth as one of the most popular knights of the Round Table. His tales revolve around his fascination with the quest of the knights, to the dismay of his wife, which prevents his return to their household. He eventually has to quest to win back her trust, a theme that plays upon the association of the King and the Goddess of the Land represented by wife or queen. The link of Morgan with Modron helps establish more divine credentials for the popular villainess of the tale, returning her domain to the blessed isles and the faery ladies.

Morgan's sister, Morgause, also has an interesting goddess connection. She is listed as Anna in the earlier works, much like Ana or Anu of the Irish. She is Arthur's sister as well, along with Morgan and Elaine, reducing the myth from nine faery sisters to three mortal sisters.

Morgause's husband is Lot, an enemy of Arthur's and they are said to have five sons, including Gawain, Agravaine, Gaheris, Fareth, and the most infamous, Mordred. This five-fold nature for those in occult circles is an interesting symbol. Five is the number of Mars in some systems, for necessary destruction and power, but the number of Venus in others system, symbolizing love. The figures range from the best to the worst Camelot has to offer. Gawain goes on to become one of the greatest knights of the Round Table. Mordred brings about the downfall of Camelot. When relating Morgause and Morgan as potential goddess figures, it shows the spectrum of life they offer, from the blessings down to the baneful.

Gawain is the most heroic of the siblings. His power is almost mythic in proportion, said to wax with the rising of the Sun and wane with its fading. Skilled in herbcraft, he can use plants to heal, giving himself some of the associations of a wise or cunning man. He is the champion of women in the stories of Camelot yet paired with no maiden. It was believed his love was of the royal families of the spirit world. Because of his many odd associations and adventures, but particularly for his solar attributes, some relate him to the Irish demi-god Cu Cuhulainn.

His best known story involves the mystery of the Green Knight. He faces a mysterious opponent, completely green from armor to skin and hair, who offers Gawain to give him any blow, if he can return it in a year and a day. Gawain beheads him, only to find the Green Knight capable of picking up his own head, and makes his appointment in a year's time. Gawain quests to keep his appointment, learning much about chivalry and honor upon the way, and makes his way to the Green Chapel to find the knight. While three blows are given, the Green Knight does not behead Gawain, but reveals his identity as a King whom he met on the adventures already, and the whole plot was a scheme devised by Morgan Le Fey to cause trouble in Camelot.

The other siblings are less honorable and adventurous. Agravaine becomes a traitor. Gaheris actually kills his mother, catching her in bed with Lamorak, but allows his siblings to believe Lamorak was the killer until his lies are revealed. Gareth is a noble and good knight, yet he does not quest in the manner of Gawain.

The villain of the tales, if there is a villain to be found along with the later incarnations of Morgan, would be Mordred. Mordred is the bastard son of Morgause and her brother Arthur, conceived when they were unaware of their relationship to each other. This very fact seems to taint him as something "wrong" and destined to poison the otherwise pure land, yet his conception is just a symptom of deeper problems beneath the surface of Camelot. He was born on May Day, and it was prophesized that a child born on this day would be the downfall of Arthur. Mordred eventually becomes the downfall of Camelot, and mortally wounds his father King Arthur, necessitating his evacuation to Avalon, where he will "rise again." In the tales where Morgan is the villain, Mordred is often her pawn. In the popular work *The Mists of Avalon* by Marion Zimmer Bradley, Morgan is actually Mordred's mother, not Morgause.

As the Morrighan has been equated with Anu and Danu, the mother of the Tuatha pantheon, Sorita d'Este and David Rankine point out in their book, *The Guises of the Morrigan*, that these gods could just as easily have been called the Tuatha de Morrigu, and all be considered children of the Morrighan. When descending upon Ireland, they are described as black birds, like the crows of the Morrighan. It makes all her interactions with the gods of the Tuatha as mother and teacher, rather than fellow, possibly illuminating different truths in her purpose and motivation.

Today, many priestesses and priests of the Morrighan, along with deeply attuned admirers and devotees of the Morrighan refer to themselves as her children, despite a general lack of mythic progeny from the Morrighan proper. Still, such devotion shows a connection to this goddess as mother as well as lover and phantom queen.

Child of the Goddess Journey

Set the mood of your journey. Hallow your space with the circle-casting techniques or by simply honoring the four directions. Light any candles you prefer, though two candles, one black and the other gray (or white) before you, with three green candles behind the first two would be appropriate. They symbolize the colors of the twins, the horses of Lugh, and then the three serpents of green. Light any incense and wear any oils that are appropriate. Use any music you like. Recite the evocation below or compose your own. Close your eyes and relax your body with every breath. Chant internally the name of the goddess "Mor-Ri-Ghan", or in this case, that of her child Meich.

To the Dark Lady Anu,
To Badb Catha,
To Macha,
To Nemain
To the Morrighan

I seek to be reborn through you,
A Tuatha de Morrigu.
I seek to be like a child to the mother
Learn as a warrior
And grow wise as a sorcerer/sorceress of the mysteries.
Awaken my hearts to you.
Beannacht! (Bahn-ukht)

In your mind's eye, envision the World Tree in the center of the Emerald Isle. This is the great oak. Pass through the thin veil and stand before it. Hear the wind in the branches. Smell the rich earth where the roots dig deep. Reach out and touch the bark, feeling the texture. Look for an opening within the roots, a tunnel that will guide you onward. Go through that tunnel and feel it spiraling below and within, to the depths of the underworld.

Come out into a clearing within a large stone circle before you. In fact, there might be several circles intertwined with each other. The rings of the stone circles are like snakes crossing over each other in a tangled knotwork pattern. They are reminiscent of a Celtic knot, or the origin of the Druid's egg. According to the scholar Pliny, a group of snakes would amass in a tangled knot and within their union form a magickal egg. If the egg could be obtained by catching it as it rose up out of the serpents and eluding the pursuing snakes, it would grant vast magickal power. As you follow the path of the stone circles, arcing back and forth, you think of the snakes. You see spirals carved into the stones from some long ago time, single spirals, double spirals and triple spirals.

In the distance, following a different arc of another circle, you see your twin, glowing in a gray or white light. Everything you do, the twin does, your mirror image. You watch your twin as you keep moving on the paths. Your twin is watching you.

Eventually the paths converge in the center of the stone complex, and you meet your twin self, your double, face to face. Like looking into a differently colored mirror, you are fascinated. And your twin is fascinated by you. You are two different perspectives of the same being, meeting in this place of stone and snake.

You reach out to your twin, and when you both touch, you merge. Instantly you are transported to darkness, into a cavernous temple cave with three bloody and beating hearts suspended in the air before you. Each is a heart of Meich. Each is a heart of the Morrighan.

Reach out to one of the hearts. Whose heart is it? From the heart comes a serpent. What does the serpent do? Accept the blessing and the wisdom of the serpent. It may be venom or words of wisdom, but in its own way, it will grant you gnosis.

In turn, choose a second heart. Release its serpent and experience its mystery.

Lastly choose the final heart and release the last of the serpents. Experience what it has to offer you.

See a light of bright white in the distance, above and beyond. You walk upward towards it. As you come out into the light, you are reborn, from the tomb temple to emerge from the womb cave. As you walk into the light, up and out from the base of the World Tree, you have a pronounced shadow, your dark twin, following you yet ever joined to you. The two are one within you. The twins are reunited in light and darkness.

Pass through the veil and leave the tree behind. Thank it for the journey and let it fade away. Return your awareness to your breath and body. Feel your limbs. Take three deep breaths and exhale strongly. Open your eyes and focus on the world of form. Ground yourself as necessary. Extinguish your candles and incense. Turn off any music. Journal your experience.

LOVERS

The Dagda is well and truly one of the best examples of the Morrighan's lovers. On Samhain, just before the Tuatha de Dannan's battle with the Fomorians, the Dagda sought out the Morrighan. As a goddess of battle, she would have the most sound strategy, and if she favored the Tuatha, then her blessing could tip the scale in their favor for victory. The Dagda finds the goddess washing herself astride the Unius River, with one foot on each shore. Both being of immense stature, they were able to couple together, and did so. The purpose of this union is not always clear. Was it a form of worship or honor to the goddess, an opportunity of union and blessing that Cu Cuhulainn missed by rejecting her later, but which the Dagda, as a full-blooded god, was wise enough to accept? Was it part of the Scorpionic energies of Samhain, in this liminal place between shores, filled with sex and the promise of death? Sex and death are the keys to understanding Scorpio, and Samhain in the northern hemisphere falls while the Sun occupies the fixed sign of Scorpio. Samhain is a critical point for the Celtic tradition, and this occasion is often noted in modern Witches' Samhain rituals. Does the sex represent some sort of pact between the Tuatha and the Morrighan, who at times appears to be one of them, and then again separate, a force that must be sought out and courted? In any case, he does succeed in gaining her favor. She promises to kill a Fomorian king and use his blood and vitality to bless the Tuatha in this war. She advises the Dagda in the war and he returns to his people.

While some would think of Cu Cuhulainn as potential lover of the Morrighan, he rightly is not so, as he did not reciprocate her advances, seemingly causing his misfortunes as far as she was concerned. He never takes the opportunity to truly be a lover, and therefore, does not receive her blessing in the way the Dagda did.

Morgan Le Fey is associated with many lovers over the many stories of Camelot. She is wife to King Uriens and either bears him a son, or raises his son as her own. Some say she takes the role that has belonged to Viviane/Nimue, and is his apprentice and lover and is later imprisoned. She learns her magick from the great mage and then uses it to trap him away from the world. That story was best popularized by the movie *Excalibur*. In *The Mists of Avalon*, she is the mother of Mordred by her half-brother Arthur. Merlin and Arthur demonstrate a later attitude of potential manipulation with sex, and paint for us a better picture of how Morgan was later thought of, rather than any ancient Pagan associations with the goddess.

Lover of the Goddess Vision

As with the Child of the Morrighan vision, set the appropriate mood for your journey with incense, music and candles. Two red candles would be appropriate for both the lover and warrior aspects of this goddess. Create a sacred space and entrance yourself after reciting this invocation or something similar:

To the Lady of the River
To the Lady of the Waters
To the Dark Lady Eternal of the Land
Morrighan
Lover of Gods and Mortals
Teacher to Heroes and Kings
I offer my love and I seek your love.
Blessings be upon us all.

Envision the World Tree in the center of the Emerald Isle, the great oak. Pass through the veil that separates you and stand before the tree. Hear the wind in the branches. Smell the rich earth where the roots dig deep. Reach out and touch the bark, feeling the bumps. Look for an opening within the roots, a tunnel that will lead you to the Morrighan. Move through the tunnel as it descends deeper and deeper.

You hear the flow of water, first as a trickle. As you move out of the tunnel, you hear the flow of water, like a stream or river. You move in the dark, following the sound until there is enough ambient light in the darkness to lead you to the banks of a river. Follow the river.

In the distance, you see the figure of a giant, wading in the river, between both shores. As you come closer, you feel the presence of the Morrighan, waiting for you in the river, beckoning you to come between. She welcomes you with open arms and open heart.

Commune with the goddess here in this place below and between. Share yourself with the goddess, as she shares her love with you. Be engulfed by the mystery of her love.

You awaken upon the mound at the base of the world tree, having risen up through the caverns of the underworld to the place of form, shape and time without memory. Stand up and thank the mighty oak. Slip back through the veil, closing it behind you. Let the world tree fade. Bring your awareness back to the realm of your flesh and blood. Take three deep breaths and exhale strongly. Open your eyes. Ground yourself as necessary. Extinguish your candles and incense. Turn off any music. Journal your experience.

HUSBANDS

Husbands of the goddess are special indeed. They transform the relationship from the privacy of children and lover, the realms of the Fifth House in astrology where Ego is built and destroyed, and move the energy of the relationship to the Seventh House. Through public declaration of the relationship, and lasting commitment, the energy is working in the House of Partnerships. Ask anyone after a long courting period as lovers: the act of marriage can change the relationship in unexpected ways due to this shift. One of the key spiritual teachings from the Morrighan is the relationship between the King, in this case husband, and the Goddess of Sovereignty. It is through the blessings of the goddess that the king rules, and he only retains that blessing when he rules wisely for not only himself, but more importantly for the people, honoring his relationship with the land and the spirit world.

Macha of the Tuatha de Dannan was possibly the wife of Nuada, a King of the Tuatha. Nuada was the first king of the Tuatha, and the king in place when they arrived in Ireland. Nuada held one of the four treasures of the Tuatha, brought from the sacred isles around the world. The Sword of Nuada is the sword of light and truth held by the king. It became the model for later famous swords, such as Excalibur. It was said that no one could resist the sword, and no one could escape it once the sword was unsheathed. During their first battle with the Fir Bolgs, he lost an arm and subsequently lost his kingship. All kings must be perfect, at least physically, and such a physical loss disqualified him for continued reign. Nuada's kingship ended and King Bres, a prince who was half-Fomorian, gained the title. Bres evidently sided with his Fomorian people, and imposed great hardship on the Tuatha. He ruled for seven years, until Nuada's arm was replaced by a magickal silver arm, and then eventually a flesh and blood arm, and he continued his rule. The removal of Bres began the Fomorian war. Nuada eventually stepped down from leadership to allow Lugh the chance to lead the Tuatha against the Fomorians. Both Nuada and Macha were killed in this war, but avenged by Lugh who then killed Balor of the Evil Eye.

Nuada really exemplifies the best match for a force like Macha. He is a power in his own right, and appears to always be working for the good of his people and the land upon which they settled. While not the Morrighan's husband specifically, Nuada, along with the Dagda and Lugh, really embody the heart of leadership and power in the Tuatha. While the Dagda is not a king, he appears much like an elder statesmen, a titanic force that is benevolently positioned toward the Tuatha. He is a lover of the Morrighan directly, and in the Celtic traditions I learned (drawing from modern inspiration) we look to the Dagda and Danu as primal father and mother. She was the mother of the children, and in many ways he was the father. If Morrighan can be equated with Danu, then this pairing can make a lot of sense. Nuada is in the world more, and takes an active leadership role and a wife, and Macha herself, in all her incarnations, is a little more accessible in the world than the Morrighan proper. Finally, Lugh is the youthful generation that takes over, and his eventual son/avatar goes on to have a relationship with the Morrighan in an adversarial or tutelary way.

The fearsome husband of Badb, and sometimes Nemain, is Neit, a god of war. He is the deity of fighting passionately, though one might think all the Celtic gods share that attribute. Neit was considered an equivalent to Mars in later mythologies, as Badb is linked to the Roman goddess Bellona. He is killed in the Second Battle of Moytura. Though associated with the Tuatha through marriage, he is also the grandfather of Balor, a Fomorian King. His Fomorian heritage would imply that he too was titanic in stature.

Nemed is the husband to the Second Macha. He ruled the second wave of people to inhabit Ireland, after the Partholons. His people are considered to be an elder generation of the Tuatha, their own ancestors. Nemed appears to have done the most landscaping of Ireland, into the recognizable shapes we might know today. In his era several lakes burst forth and were created.

He created two forts and cleared twelve plains. He died along with his people in a plague and was buried on the Great Island of Cork Harbor.

Crunnchu was the boastful husband of Macha, the faery wife. Out of all the husbands, he probably best demonstrates the ego of men in relationship to the goddess. She makes him promise not to speak of her, and particularly of her otherworldly status, but he makes a boast that she can outrun the King's fastest horses. The King follows his example of ego, forcing a pregnant woman to run to save the honor, and life, of her husband. For their acts of ego, insensitivity and cruelty, all the men of Ulster are cursed by Macha.

Cimbáeth is the husband of Macha Mong Ruad. Grandson of Airgetmar, along with Aed Ruad and Dithorba, they shared the role of High King of Ireland in seven-year shifts. After the death of Aed at the end of his third term, they continued the pattern. When Aed's turn came again, his daughter, Macha Mong Ruad asked for her turn at High Queenship of Ireland. She battled Dithorba and his sons, but ended up marrying Cimbáeth, presumably to cement her rule over the long term.

The Great God Vision

Sometimes the best way to understand one aspect of divinity is to encounter its complement and partner. Exploring a fierce goddess power such as the Morrighan in all her aspects is difficult. She has so many facets and faces. Trying to approach her consort's energy, the God's consciousness, can help you better understand her and your relationship with her. We often get to know a friend deeper in relationship to their spouse or partner. The question is, who is the great god who is the partner to the Morrighan? Is it Neit, the god of war? Is it one of the various husbands, immortal or mortal of Macha, such as Nuadam, Nemed, Crunnchu or Cimbáeth? While technically a lover, is the only real match for this grand goddess the figure of the Dagda, as she is seen as a more knowable face of Danu? Part of the working is for you to find how your chosen god will let you approach understanding the nature and mystery of the Morrighan.

Establish your setting with appropriate music, incense and candles. A single white, gold or red candle would be appropriate. Make sacred space and enter into trance after reciting this or something similar:

To the Great Lord
To the Great God
To the consort of the Lady Morrighan
I call upon you.

Open the way
Show me the mystery
Teach me.
So mote it be.

Conjure the World Tree before you, growing in the center of the Emerald Isle. Step through the veil of spirit that separates you from the great oak. Listen for the wind whispering in its branches. Smell the soil where the roots dig deep. Touch the bark. Feel the texture. Hold your intention of seeking the God and look for a passageway in the roots. This tunnel will lead you to the mystery that is the God.

The spiraling tunnel may seem to take you upward, within the vast tree like a corkscrew. You climb the spire toward the heavens. You see a small, distant light, and with each moment, it grows brighter and brighter. As you approach it, you find yourself enveloped in the light, bathed in its warm glow.

As the light fades, you find yourself in a paradisiacal realm of mist and soft light, much brighter and lighter than your journeys to the realms below. You find yourself on a path, and walk the path, realizing you are in a misty, lush field where everything seems perfect.

On the path in the distance is a castle or tower, some sort of structure that calls to you. You know it's your destination, and you approach it.

Take a good long gaze at the structure. What do you see? The door opens freely for you. Enter. Walk the great hall and come upon the throne of the God. Who waits there for you?

Commune with the God who resides in the castle. Ask about the nature of the Morrighan and his relationship to her. Experience the mystery of the Dark Lady from her consort. What can he teach you, and will he? What must you offer in return?

When your encounter is complete, give thanks and blessings to the God who greeted you in this castle. Follow your way out, keeping to the same path back and returning to the branches of the great tree. Follow the tunnel within the tree downward to the base of the tree. Thank the spirit of the World Tree. Pass back through the veil and let the tree fade as the veil closes behind you. Bring your attention to your flesh and blood, breath and bone as you take three deep breaths and exhale strongly. Open your eyes and ground yourself as needed. Put out your candles and incense. Turn off your music and journal your experience.

THE MORRIGHAN & THE WHEEL OF THE YEAR

As a goddess of fertility, the land, battle and death, her power is certainly evident in the turning of the life tides with the Wheel of the Year. The Wheel of the Year is a modern view of seasonal celebrations uniting the four Celtic fire festivals, considered major sabbats among Witches, with the solar festivals and the customs of the Saxons and Norse. All have been celebrated rurally in the folklore of the British Isle, and that potent mix is what modern Pagans have inherited.

For this text, we'll be focusing on only three of the eight major sabbats of Neopaganism: Lughnasadh, Mabon (Autumn Equinox) and Samhain. Each are harvest feasts, specifically of grains, fruits and meat respectively. Each attunes to the nature and some of the mythos in harmony with the Morrighan and her many aspects.

While it might be incomplete to not write about the other five sabbats, a clever practitioner will be able to draw inspiration from the brighter deities in the Celtic pantheons, and devise balanced practices to complete the wheel. Traditional Irish lore would only use the four fire festival sabbats of Samhain, Imbolc, Beltane and Lughnasadh as well, and you'll see our Mabon rite has a distinctively more Welsh and Arthurian framework, while still drawing upon the gods of many Celtic lands.

Lughnasadh

Lughnasadh (Loo-na-sa) generally is translated as "the assembly of Lugh" or "the funeral feast and games of Lugh" though it originally didn't refer to his death and funeral, but that of his mother, the Fomorian goddess Tailitu. She died clearing the fields of Ireland for agricultural use, and he instituted the funeral celebration and games, often celebrated as the Tailtean Games, in her honor. As traditions changed in the creation of modern Wicca and various Neopagan offshoots, Lugh transformed from a storm and lightning god, where light rain was a sign of his presence on this day, to a god of the Sun and grain, and the funeral became his own in the cutting of the grain. Due to the climate in Ireland, Lammas—the Saxon name of the harvest—probably had more to do with the first fruits, particularly berries, than it did grain. Rituals would be performed to prevent late summer storms from damaging the crops, as the offerings were believed to appease the god of storms. If his mother was not honored properly, there would be damaging storms. Now corn cakes and corn dolly effigies would be made and sacrificed as token of the grain god Lugh, and storms are less feared.

The holiday links to the Morrighan through the tale of Macha. While specifically in her myth, her fabled horse race simply takes place at a fair, traditions have grown around the concept that the fair was held on Lughnasadh, as horse racing plays a big part in the Lughnasadh games. Her curse comes to the men of Ulster on this holy day, making an interesting dichotomy of goddesses. Tailitu gives a gift freely to the people. Disrespected, Macha gives a curse. Lugh's descendant or avatar, Cu Chulainn, ultimately bears the brunt of the curse even though he is unaffected. He too disrespects the goddess in the form of the Morrighan and suffers for it until his ultimate death.

Today we can celebrate Lughnasadh giving honor to Tailitu, Macha and Lugh, to seek the blessings and balance of all involved in the first harvest.

Create an altar appropriate for this harvest right. Grains, bread, berries and beer or other malt beverages are appropriate. Candles of yellow and gold, as well as black and gray (or white if gray is difficult to find) are fitting.

Create sacred space and cast your circle. Call the four quarters using a set that is appropriate for you. For this ritual, I suggest these four based on the four Airts. The Airts are a Gaelic tradition of colors with the directions, and many consider them the spirits of the four directions from a distinctively Celtic, or at least British, perspective, when much of our modern Neopagan directional lore is usually rooted in more Middle Eastern traditions. Many believe a more traditional calling of the quarters for Celtic traditions, found in more of the poetry, is to move North, South, East, West, creating a cross, rather than a circle. The colors are also appropriate both for the Triple Goddess, and with the addition of gray, for Macha, as one of Cu Chulainn's horses was "Macha's Gray."

Black spirits of the midnight North
White spirits of the noon time South
Like magick words spoken, from the sacred mouth
Red spirits of the dawning East
Grey spirits of the twilight West
Come ye that may, so we are all blessed.
Throughout and about, around and around.
Our circle is drawn.
Our circle is bound.

These very simple quarter calls are adapted from a chant channeled by Doreen Valiente from an 18th century deceased Witch acting as a spirit contact of hers named John Brakespeare, and printed in her book, *The Rebirth of Witchcraft*. Here is the original chant:

Black spirits and white,
Red spirits and grey,
Come ye, come ye, come ye that may.
Throughout and about, around and around,
The circle drawn, the circle bound.

Continuing the Ritual:

By She Who is Prophet, Seeress and Sorceress
By She Who is Faery Wife, Swift Horse and Mother of Twins
By She Who is Queen, Red Braids and Conquering
We call upon you,
Macha
Of the Feathered Cloak
Macha
Of the Swiftest Horse
Macha
Of the Crown of Red Tresses
Hail and Welcome.

We call He Who Knocks on the Doors of Tara
We call upon you Lugh
Lord of Lightning and Storms
Lugh
Lord of Light and Spear
Lugh
King of Grains and Harvest.
Hail and Welcome.

And we call upon She Who Came Before
Foster Mother of Lugh

Giver of Life
Giver of Hope
And Giver of the Mourning Games
Tailitu.
Hail and Welcome.

Light your candles and any appropriate incense. Make offerings to the gods of your grains, bread and drink. If outdoors with a large fire, ideally throw them into the fire. If near a body of flowing water or sea water, put them in the water. If not, place them in nature when the rite concludes and make libations upon the ground if outdoors.

The purpose of the seasonal vision working is to reflect upon reaping what we sow, considered karma in the Eastern traditions, and Wyrd in the Germanic, but generally meaning the teaching of consequences and results on many levels. The king and men of Ulster dishonor Macha by making her race, and the seeds of their actions lie dormant for many generations, until the time of Cu Chulainn. Then the great warriors of the northern territory are struck with the pain of childbirth in their time of greatest need. Cu Chulainn disrespects the goddess as the Morrighan in her many forms. Ultimately, it brings about his end through battle. Both are considered the "negative" consequences of man in respect towards the goddess. Each was warned many times and could have changed the course of his actions.

As many turn to modern Pagan practices in an effort to redress the imbalance between humanity and the goddess, we seek to restore our relationship with the divine feminine. Many feel we are collectively in the same position as these men, being warned by nature, and not heeding the warning. Lughnasadh is a great time to work toward this restoration of balance in our hearts and minds, as we can both honor Macha and restore respect to her through honor and kindness, as well as Tailitu, a Fomorian figure responsible for fostering the great and noble Lugh and clearing the land so we may eat.

Enter your trance state through whatever method best suits you at this time. Go deep and summon forth a misty veil, like the mists of the faery lands from where Macha and the Tuatha de Dannan departed, beneath the land and waves. As the mist clears, you find yourself on the edge of a great circle, a great race track. There is a tower of Black to the North, Red to the East, White to the South and Gray to the West. Next to you are horses.

A bell is struck and you're off with the horses, running around the track. You circle around, getting faster as they get faster. You go around and around, exhausting yourself but not able to stop. You get dizzy from the circular motion around and around, but find yourself as if in a vortex, a tornado of energy battering you around. You keep circling until you find yourself in the center still point.

In the center you see the goddess as Macha transform from a horse into the magnificent dark queen that she is. She gives birth to two energies, two shapes that start out like horses, one red and one gray, then turning one black and one white, but soon they take the form of young men, of a dual young god. One is bright and light, the dawn and noon. One is darkness and twilight, sunset and midnight. They shift and morph into each other as they greet you. They speak to you of the mysteries of the twins, of duality in all things in the world of form and shape.

The three open the Earth up in the center of the spinning ring. Macha and her two sons open the way to a central stone, what the Greeks called the omphalos, the navel of the world. There holding it is Tailitu, she who moved all the small stones and fused them into this central stone, this altar, this throne. She gathered the stones and now, like the King Stone, they sit in the center. Tailitu invites you to the center of the world. Here you see all that was, all that is, and all that will be, from below, just as some goddesses show it to you from above in the stars. Here, you learn the mysteries of restoring the world and the goddess by fulfilling your own role. What must you sow? What must you sacrifice? What stones must you move? Listen with an open heart and mind.

When done, the mist rises again and you are returned from your deep trance to the circle. Take a sacrament of bread, knowing that it is here because of the many goddesses like Tailitu. Take a sacrament of beer, wine or water and drink deeply. Think about your missions to sow new seeds and tend them. Think about what you must sacrifice and separate from to fulfill this work in the world. Rest there between the worlds in the presence of the gods.

Then thank and devoke the deities.

We thank She Who is Mistress of Magick
We thanks She Who is Swifter than Horses
We thank She Who is Cunning in Battle.
We thank you Macha
For all blessings, gifts and lessons.
Hail and farewell.

We thank He Who is Many Skilled
We thank He Who is Victorious in Battle
We Thank He Who Commands Light from the Sky.

We thank you Lugh
For all blessings, gifts and lessons.
Hail and farewell.

We thank She Who Gave her Life
She Who cleared the Land
She who fostered the Light.
We thank you Tailitu
For all blessings, gifts and lessons.
Hail and farewell.

The release of the quarters is less traditional, done in reverse. While someone more attuned with Celtic Reconstructionism would simply release north, south, east and west again, my own Witchcraft background informs me of a need to do things at this point in the ritual in a reversed order, in the spirit of "deconstructing" the space.

Grey Spirit of the Twilight West
Red spirits of the dawning East
We thank you and you are released.
White spirits of the noontime south
Black spirits of the midnight north.
We thank you for faring forth.
Our circle is undone,
So fare thee well to your abodes
May we have peace as you travel
Back upon the second roads.

When you feel the four quarter spirits released, then release your magick circle and ground as necessary. Dispose of any of your offerings in nature and continue to feast on bread, fruit and beer.

CHAPTER EIGHT
The Healing Isle

In my own personal gnosis and understanding of the Goddess as the creative force and body of the universe, portrayed in the wide variety of Celtic myths inspiring Neopagans today, I find a connection between the Morrighan and Morgan Le Fey, not just in name, but in my own visions. The connecting link, strangely, is through the figure of Ceridwen. The one thing they all have in common is that these figures are all Ladies of the Isle, if not all Ladies of the Lake.

Considered a goddess today in Neopagan circles, Ceridwen is explicitly stated as a Witch or enchantress. We tend to assume that she has a goddess stature, though it is really implied, as with many figures of the Celtic legends. At first glance, she has very little to do with the Morrighan or Morgan Le Fey, though looking at her story helped me understand the nature of my connection to the Goddess in her greatest aspect, and specifically helped develop my relationship with Morrighan through both healing and challenges.

Ceridwen and her giant husband, Tegid Voel, made their home on Lake Bala on an island in the center of the lake. Upon the island was her hut, and within her hut was a magick cauldron. The cauldron was the cauldron of inspiration, capable of brewing a wondrous potion. Ceridwen and Tegid had two children, a beautiful girl as bright as daylight known as Creirwy, and a dark son named Morfran. Morfran was unloved by others, frightened by his dark appearance covered with dark fur or according to some, black feathers. He was so fearsome, he was also called Afagddu, or Utter Darkness. Ceridwen, being a Witch, tried to use her magick to make her son as beautiful as her daughter, but it did not work. In her wisdom, she decided if she could not change his outer form, she would change his inner form, granting him eloquence, wisdom and magick through the power of inspiration, of awen. Then people would love and adore him despite his looks.

The potion's formula was complex and required constant care. She would have to travel the world to find the ingredients. She gathered two servants to her. The first was the blind man Morda, who tended the fire beneath the cauldron, keeping it the perfect temperature, not too hot and not too cool. She also got the young boy Gwion Bach to constantly stir the cauldron day and night. Together, Morda and Gwion worked in the dark hut, lit only by firelight. Ceridwen would come and go, traveling the world, gathering her herbs and ingredients at the proper astrological day and hour. She would add her herbs, one by one over the course of a year and a day, instructing Gwion to stir them in.

One day, just before the year and a day was complete, Morda let the fire get too hot. The brew of awen began to steam and boil. Gwion continued to stir it, and three drops flew out of the cauldron and burned his thumb as he stirred. By instinct he sucked his thumb to stop the pain, and in those three drops, imbibed all the magick of the potion. The remainder turned to poison, cracked the cauldron and flowed out of the hut, into the lake and down the river to a weir. At the weir, Gwyddno's horses were drinking. They drank the poison and died.

Gwion immediately knew that Ceridwen would know what happened and be so furious she would kill him, so he escaped from the hut and the island. He used his new wisdom to shapeshift into an animal he thought would make the fastest getaway, a hare. Cerdiwen made her way back to her island and became a greyhound to capture him. Just before the greyhound's jaws snapped at the hare, Gwion jumped into the river and became a salmon, swimming away. Ceridwen followed him as an otter and caught up with him. Just as the otter grabbed the salmon, the salmon shifted his shape again, jumping out of the river and becoming a wren. Ceridwen followed suit, becoming a hawk, chasing the wren. Just as the wren would be caught, Gwion eyed a granary, and saw the threshing room floor covered with grain. He changed tactics and became a single grain and hid among the other grain. Ceridwen became a black hen, and ate them all. Soon she realized that she was pregnant with the light of Gwion, and would give birth to him in nine months.

She did give birth nine months later, and while still furious, she found she could not kill the babe she gave birth to, but she couldn't keep him as a constant reminder of her failure to her poor ugly son. She placed him in a leather satchel and called upon fate, casting him upon the waters. The satchel was caught in the weir on Beltane day, and fishing in the weir was Gwyddno, seeking salmon. He found the satchel, opened it and the light of the Sun struck the brow of the golden child. Gwyddno proclaimed, "Taliesin!" The child said, "Golden brow you say, golden brow I shall be," and was thus named Taliesin. The infant spoke, sang and prophesized, becoming the chief bard of Gwyddno's household and then the entire land. Ceridwen was then known as Mother of the Bards.

Ceridwen's origin? We are uncertain. Though in the second branch of the Mabiongi, Branwen Daughter of Llyr, featuring Bran and Branwen and their own Cauldron of Rebirth, Bran states in a conversation with King Matholwch that he obtained the Cauldron from two giants, Llassar Llaegyvnewid and Kymideu Kymeinvoll, living on a lake, who escaped from Ireland and fled to Wales, giving him the vessel.

And a second night sat they together. "My lord," said Matholwch, "whence hadst thou the cauldron which thou hast given me?" "I had it of a man who had been in thy land," said he, "and I would not give it except to one from there." "Who was it?" asked he. "Llassar Llaesgyvnewid; he came here from Ireland with Kymideu Kymeinvoll, his wife, who escaped from the Iron House in Ireland, when it was made red hot around them, and fled hither.

– *The Mabinogion,* translated by Lady Charlotte Guest

This links the magick of this Welsh cauldron to the Irish, to a gigantic couple, and possibly to Ceridwen and Tegid Voel. Many believe these figures to be Irish Tuatha de Dannan who came to Wales, and the sound of the name Kymideu has some resonance with Ceridwen. While not a direct connection to the Morrighan, it is a connection to her people and to the island, to Ériu, the emerald gem of the western sea. She is either the embodiment of the land itself, or came with the Tuatha from other mysterious islands beyond the known shores. Interestingly enough, her natural son Morfran or Morvran, is sometimes translated as Great Crow or Sea Crow, making a connection to the Morrighan. Ceridwen gives birth to a crow boy. He is described as being black, possibly with feathers. Despite his misfortune with Gwion Bach, Morfran goes on to have his own career as a warrior and possibly a poet or bard, and it was said that none would strike him because they feared by his dark looks that he was the Devil.

We can look at Ceridwen as Wales' first Lady of the Lake, first sorceress and mistress of the herbs, while Morgan Le Fey is a later incarnation of such a figure for the Arthurian time and mythos. Closer to our own time, we can have a greater understanding of how our time and spiritual culture relate to the lady on the island. The time of the Arthurian mythos, while distant and mythical, for our modern visions of Camelot never quite existed, does paint a scene that is a remarkable blend of cultures and beliefs, not unlike our own world today.

Britain has been the melting pot for so many of our western magickal traditions. By the time of Arthur it had the oldest layers of the Stone Age people overlaid with the Celts, then Romans and finally the Saxon invasions. Structures, gods, beliefs, language, art and culture all mixed and influenced what would become England. Today we can add the movements of Christianity, alchemy, Qabalah, Sufism, eastern mysticism via the Theosophical society, spiritualism and ceremonial magick to the cauldron of the British Isles. Even more vast is the melting pot, the cauldron of magick with the addition of New Age thought, Reiki, and Native American movements imported to Britain. As we can relate to the time of Arthur in his own cultural mixing pot, we tend to relate to the mystery of the island in the same way: Avalon.

THE FORTUNATE ISLE

Avalon, the land of apples and in particular, healing, has fascinated our modern retellings of the story. One of the most popular "new" contributions to the Arthurian mythos is the pro-feminine *The Mists of Avalon* by Marion Zimmer Bradley. It's become a staple in many Celtic-influenced Witchcraft groups today. Avalon is an otherworldly refuge for Paganism, for magick, for healing and for the goddess. It has allegories in other mythologies, most notably the land of Tír na nÓg, the Land of Youth in Irish mythology. Sometimes it's depicted as an Island in the West, or the land beneath the hills and water where the Tuatha de Dannan, including the Morrighan, reside after the coming of the Milasians. In Greek mythology, the island is depicted as Hesperides. Within it, there is a garden sacred to Hera, with a tree that gives golden apples. The apple reference is similar to Avalon, and heroes of Greek myth such as Hercules are charged to gain the apples. Other traditions look to the western isles as Atlantis, with a possibility of the

Canary Islands being a remnant of the fabled island continent. The Atlantean myth, while similar, has some marked differences, not being a paradise island, but a land where power eventually corrupts, and modern mystics look to Atlantis with a mythic nostalgia. Buyan is the Slavic mythic island where the spirits and gods reside. In general, the islands are referred to as the Blessed Isle, or Fortune Isles, and are known for their wide range of birds and luscious fruit.

In the Welsh tradition, the most direct source of the Arthurian lore, it was known as Ynys Afallach, meaning the Island of Apples, and eventually Affalon and then the more familiar Avalon. Avalon has been most famously associated with a district of England known today as Glastonbury, known for its very high spiritual energy due to the intersection of ley lines through an earth mound known as the Tor. Another name for the area was Ynys Gutrin, the Island of Glass, and eventually the Saxons came up with the name Galstingebury, or Glastonbury. Glass and crystal, and the clarity of such waters compared to glass, are strongly associated with the otherworld. Mirrors and reflections often form a veil between our world and that of the spirits. Such imagery is found in many cultures and traditions. Glass implies that it is present, right there with you, but it is transparent. It can only be perceived under certain conditions. Otherwise, things pass right through it.

A mix of Pagan and Christian ways exist upon the land today, with the agricultural tiers of the Tor interpreted as an ancient Pagan labyrinth, and a tower dedicated to St. Michael, as well as a chapel in the Abbey to the Irish St. Bridget, who reportedly visited there. There is also a small mound associated with Bridget. Various astrological alignments can be found by using the various mounds and Tor of Glastonbury. Many today believe the Tor was surrounded by swampy water, and the top of it formed the Island we know of as Avalon, while what is now the town of Glastonbury was the island, with the areas surrounding Glastonbury submerged beneath the brackish water.

While divided into three separate sections, the workings of this chapter, the *Journey of the Glass Boat*, the *Sword of Light* and the *Healing Grail of Avalon* can be done in sequence, one right after the other, without breaking trance. Read the entire chapter, then go back and do the workings. If necessary you can also do them individually to attune to each of the specific parts of the teaching.

Journey of the Glass Boat Vision

Establish your ritual setting with all the appropriate tools you have learned and make sacred space. Evoke the blessings of Avalon for safe passage:

By the Water and Fires of Avalon
I seek entry into the Fortunate Isle.
I seek safe passage into the Isle of Glass.
I seek the magick of the Isle of Apples.
Please open the way for my intention is pure.
Blessed be.

Call forth the mist. Call forth the misty veil that separates us from Avalon, as if the white clouds are rising up out of the ground itself to surround you. Feel yourself immersed in the glowing white mist.

The mists part just before you, and you hear the swirling of water, like the tide coming in. One of the nine sisters, one of the nine priestess queens of Avalon, comes before you in an invisible, magickal boat. You see her clearly sitting above the water, beckoning you to join her, but you cannot see the spirit boat. She holds out her hand for you to enter. Grasp her hand and join her in the glass boat, the spirit chariot that shall take you through the mist and across the water.

The boat mysteriously pushes off, and you gaze through the bottom at the waters. Are they clear like crystal or are they murky? Do you see anything in the waters?

You go deeply into the mist and can only see the silhouette of your traveling companion. She is speaking to you, but perhaps in a language you do not know. You feel the power, the vibration of her words. They are soothing and healing and take you deeper into your trance. As she speaks, her shape might shift. What does she become?

The boat gently strikes the shore, and she beckons you to get out upon the beach. There you wander the Isle of Avalon. The land seems to be insubstantial, a dream or spirit vision. You are clearly there, but you are not sure where "there" is. The landscape shifts and morphs as you turn. It does not stay solid, except that there is the general sense that it ascends to a high point in the center. There are trees and orchards, and of course, apples in both flower and a fruit at the same time. There are magnificent rows of ancient oak trees and hawthorn trees, also both in white flower and red berry. Beware of their sharp spikes.

Wander the Isle of Glass and see who you meet. Perhaps your ferrywoman will guide you further, or leave you to your own exploration.

When done, either continue onward to seek the sword of light, or ask your guide to return you to the world of shape and form.

The Sword of the Island

Though many would not suspect a weapon to be associated with Avalon, the legendary sword of King Arthur was supposedly forged in Avalon, imbuing it with magickal powers beyond those of an ordinary sword.

Originally known as *Caledfwlch* in Welsh, Excalibur is not the same as the Sword in the Stone that most people casually familiar with the Camelot myth would know. Though some accounts do equate them, usually they are seen as two very different swords. At one point, the Sword from the Stone is broken, and Merlin takes Arthur to the Lady of the Lake to receive a new one. He receives a magick sword that can cut through steel and stone like wood, but more importantly, the scabbard possesses magickal powers. Anyone who had the scabbard could not die from blood loss. Some accounts would even say anyone with the scabbard who received a wound would not even bleed. In the accounts where Morgan Le Fey is the villain, she steals the scabbard and usually throws it into a lake, losing it forever.

While the overt magickal properties are mighty, the deeper significance of the sword relates to the Sword of Nuada, one of the four treasures of the Tuatha de Dannan. The Arthurian mythos, ripe with both Pagan and Christian symbolism, is loaded with images that correspond to the four hallows of the Tuatha that have become such standard symbolism in western magick, Tarot and Witchcraft.

Claiomh Solais is the name of the Sword of Nuada, also known as the Sword of Light for it glowed with the light of the Sun. No one could resist its power in battle and it could cleave its enemies in two. The sword of light belonged to the king of the Tuatha de Dannan, just as Excalibur belonged to King Arthur, rightful ruler of Britain. The sword somehow symbolizes the role of the male priest to the terrestrial and abyssal powers of the world through the Mother Goddess. It is a badge or vestment of office.

In modern western magick, the sword is usually associated with the element of air and its highest principle, truth. Those who hold the magician's sword wisely, hold their true power of words and their own truth. The words they speak come true. They can bind and command spirits and make worlds move.

For us, modern magickal workers seeking the mystery of the Morrighan and her various guises as the Ladies of the Lake, we must be in relationship with the planet to find our own sovereignty. To be truly sovereign, we must be true. We must live true to our word. We must be honorable. We must understand the power of our words and judgments. If we do not, we cannot rule our own lives with integrity. Seeking the Lady for this vestment, this tool of our own office, to rule as the secret king or queen of our life is a very important step. Those who guard the whole power of the sword, blade and scabbard, find a bit of immorality in spirit, if not always the flesh.

Sword of Light Vision

Upon the Glass Isle, you are drawn to a light upon a small hill. A larger hill, a Tor, looms in the distance, but at the base of this larger hill is a smaller, rounded mound with a light emanating from the mist. You are drawn to that light.

There before you is a blacksmith priestess, striking an anvil with a hammer, tempering some tool or weapon. The light is coming not from a furnace, but from a well.

The forge priestess welcomes you, and shows you that the furnace for her work is the fire that flows, the water that burns, the mysteries of life. Fire from water is her secret, for the swords of light are forged beneath the waters of love. Truth is tempered by love, and then it shines with a power that cannot be denied. Love and truth are not ours exclusively. They are offered. They are lived. But ultimately they are from the divine, and to the divine they must return. We wield them as tools. They help us as allies, but they are not us, and we are not them. They are part of our regimen while we seek our sovereignty in this world.

The priestess holds up a Sword of Light. Its glow is dazzling. Gaze into the light. Let the light commune with you. Feel the light. Listen to any message it might have for you in words, vision or intuition. Become one with the light. There is no separation between you and it.

When done, the priestess might tell you to take the sword, and possibly a scabbard to go with it, or tell you what you must do to truly earn the sword and return for it. This Lady of the Lake guides you onward.

If you feel your experience is complete, return the way you came, or go onward to the Healing Grail of Avalon.

The Healing Grail

Along with the Sword, the most popular item associated with the Isle of Avalon is the Holy Grail. Harkening back to the cauldron of Ceridwen and her great potion of inspiration, the myth is transformed again with the rise of Christianity. The Cauldron of the goddess is transformed into the cup of the Last Supper of Christ and hidden in Avalon.

Many of the Christian traditions get wrapped up in the lore of Avalon and Glastonbury. Many Christian saints supposedly visited Glastonbury, and there is even one myth of Jesus visiting the British Isles as a child to study with the Druids, following the tin traders with his uncle. Joseph of Arimathea visited Glastonbury with the Holy Grail in hand, and supposedly planted the Hawthorn Tree on Wearyall Hill by driving in his walking stick. He placed the Grail itself in the Red Well, where it then flowed with the "red" waters of Christ's blood. In actuality, the red comes from an iron deposit, though the waters have a reputation for remarkable healing in both Pagan and Christian traditions. There is a matching white spring, rich with calcium, that also has healing properties, which shows the two important colored waters in the western British traditions, red and white. These colors are found in the myths of Merlin and his two dragons, and in the native British with the red dragon and invading Saxons with the white dragon.

In the Arthurian mythos, the land is blighted by various betrayals, depending on the version of the story, and the Knights of the Round Table must quest to find the Holy Grail, as the grace of God and virtue of Christ through the Grail can restore the land and the King. A knight must simply be worthy of finding it and thereby the land will be worthy of being healed. There is a reciprocal relationship between the quest and the result. In many ways, the journey is more important than the destination. The knights search far and wide, though never in the ever-elusive Avalon, but those knights with the strongest otherworldly associations are usually the most successful of the Grail Knights in the various stories. Modern Pagans feel that beneath the Christian overlay there is a deeper mystery of the sacrificial cults of kingship and their relationship to the otherworld.

The counterpart to the Lady of the Lake in Avalon is the Fisher King or Wounded King, residing in his castle next to the river. He is eternally wounded in the thigh, or genitals, symbolizing his lack of virility to spiritually fertilize the land. While Avalon is a place of healing, Castle Corbenic is a place of testing, to see who is worthy of the Grail. The knight must only make it to the castle, meet with the King, seek the grail and ask, "Whom does the Grail serve?"

In my own spiritual work, in vision I've encountered the grail in different ways at the Isle of Avalon from the Red Well and in the Castle Corbenic. For our work on the Healing Isle and the Ladies of the Lake, we shall focus on the vision of Avalon as a place of healing freely given. Though not associated directly with the Arthurian stories, but in my own exploration of the Morrighan, you can encounter the crows of Avalon, those who will draw out that which no longer serves to make room within for the healing waters of the goddess's grail.

Healing Grail of Avalon Vision

You are guided to the Healing Temple of the Glass Isle, where the chief priestess and Lady of the Lake resides. Enter the temple and you might be overwhelmed by the sights and smells. Various herbs hang and incenses burn in this temple, affecting the body, mind, heart and soul.

The dark-robed lady ushers you in and she too might speak in a language that makes no linear sense as well, but the vibration is very soothing to you. These are words of power and healing. She urges you to lie down upon a healing table. Do so and as you gaze up, you realize that the temple has no roof, just four walls, like the Tower of Saint Michael. You start thinking about the issues of your life that are in need of healing, ranging from the physical to the spiritual.

She calls down the crows and ravens of Avalon. They fly down and land upon your body and the table. The crows begin to peck at you, but do not cause any pain. They start pulling out any illnesses, worries, and harmful energy. They are carrion feeders, and they feed on "dis-ease" of any kind like rotting flesh. Their eating makes room for new flesh, new energy, new thoughts and feelings to grow without infection by the old and ill.

When done with their work, the crows en mass flock away upward through the Temple. The lady gently helps you rise and as you sit up, she gives you a cup of bright red liquid. Drink from the cup. Take this living life force into your body. Feel it tingle with warmth. Feel it burn ever so slightly as it goes down. Feel its warmth fill in all the spaces that were made by the crows. Feel yourself become more healthy and whole. Thank the dark lady of the lake.

One of the attending priestesses to the Lady of the Lake then enters. She helps you to your feet and guides you back down the hill. She helps you to the shifting beach and to the invisible boat. Your ferrywoman is waiting for you, to return you to where you began in the mist. She guides you through the mist, and you can gaze below to the water. How does the water look to you now?

You reach the shore, and she again gently beckons you to disembark as the mists close once again around her. She fades away in the mist. Soon the mists fade away from you, leaving you in the realm of shape and form, of solidness and time. Give thanks and blessing again. Take three deep breaths to center yourself in the world. Open your eyes and ground yourself. Release your sacred space and return to normal by extinguishing any remaining candles or incense. Take this time to journal about your healing experience.

MABON

Out of all the eight Neopagan holidays of the Wheel of the Year, the autumn equinox, known as Mabon, is the one most strongly associated with Apples, Avalon and King Arthur. The story of Mabon involves this child of Light, Mabon ap Modron, the son of Modron the Mother Goddess, a cognate of Danu in Welsh mythology. Born without a father, Mabon gets lost in the darkness of the other world or is kidnapped at only three days old. In the most popular version of the story, it is King Arthur and his knights who rescue him, going to the eldest creatures of the world and asking their wisdom. Each animal gives its wisdom, but suggests the questing knights go to the wisdom of the previous age with a different animal. They visit the blackbird, the stag, the owl, the eagle and the salmon. While it's a quest for a child, it is also a journey into the wisdom of the Earth and Underworld, into our ancestral past, and to the wisdom of the animals.

While not explicitly stated, the world where Mabon is held prisoner is the Otherworld, the realm of the depths, with links to the lands of Elphame and Avalon. He is kept in the Castle or Keep of Gloucester. While a city in England, it is usually considered by those in occultism not to be the terrestrial Gloucester found on a map, but a spirit world where the light of the God has been taken, bringing darkness to the land. While confined to the keep, he sings through the walls, leading the knights to him. His lament is reminiscent of faery songs of folklore.

In the modern Witch's understanding of the Wheel of the Year, the tale of Mabon has been grafted upon the celebration of the Autumn Equinox. Celebrated by many as a time of Thanksgiving, the spiritual concept at this station on the Wheel of the Year is the descent from life to death, the shift of the balance point towards darkness. To the modern Witch, Mabon, the God, descends like light into the darkness, to return to the womb of the mother for rest and regeneration, to be reborn. We all need our time to return to the darkness, to return to the Mother, for rest and regeneration.

While she is the goddess who loses her child, she is also the goddess who receives the child. She is the queen of the depths. Like the Queen of Avalon, she empowers the child of light, in the Arthurian mythos seen as Arthur with the sword Excalibur, and she receives him again into darkness, as Arthur returns to Avalon to heal and slumber.

Mabon Ritual

Prepare a suitable Mabon altar. Apples are an appropriate decoration for this ritual. Red and white are appropriate colors for altar cloths and other decorations. Have the Morrighan Elixir prepared as a sacrament for the chalice. Burn Morgana the Faery Queen Incense and use Faery

Queen oil. This can be done as a group ritual, with various quarter callers playing the roles of the five elder animals, or done in solitary journey.

Breathe deeply and enter a light trance state. Cast your circle to create sacred space. Use whatever quarter calls you desire, or try these specifically for the Mabon ritual, based upon the animals associated with his story.

To the powers of the North, we call upon the element of Earth and the Stag. We call you to this circle. Hail and welcome.

To the powers of the East, we call upon the element of Fire and the Owl. We call you to this circle. Hail and welcome.

To the powers of the South, we call upon the element of Air and the Eagle. We call you to this circle. Hail and welcome.

To the powers of the West, we call upon the element of Water and the Salmon. We call you to this circle. Hail and welcome.

Complete the circle, returning to the North. Circle back to the front of the altar, acknowledge Spirit by saying:

And Spirit, with the Blackbird, always with us, So mote it be.

Light a candle for the Goddess and a candle for the God, with this evocation:

I call to the Goddess, the Mother, the Source of All Enchantments and Life
Danu, Morrighan, Modron, Rhiannon, Arianrhod, Ceridwen, Morgana
I call to you.
Hail and welcome.

I call to the God, the Father, the Giver of Life, Death and Blessings
Dagda, Nuada, Nudd, Pywll, Gwydion, Tegid, Arthur
I call to you.
Hail and welcome.

We call to the child of light within us Lugh, Mabon, Gwyn, Lleu, Taleisin, Pryderi
Oh Child of Promise, please show us the light in the darkness

And guide our way in the mysteries
As we turn the Wheel of the Year towards the dark.

Anoint yourself and others participating with oil. Perform the sacrament. Take your wand or blade and draw to it with your Will the light of the heavens and depths. With that golden point of light at the tip, plunge it within the elixir held within the chalice.

By the most ancient of ancients,
We seek blessings in this place and time.
Open the way.
So mote it be.

Pour out a libation on the ground, or if indoors, in a libation bowl to later be returned to the Earth and drink your fill, feeling the magick of the light within the elixir.

The Lord of Light has been slain, cut down with the first grain upon the threshing floor. His golden spirit is returned to the underworld like a newborn child, awaiting return. We must usher the spirit of our Lord to the Womb of the Mother. We guide him as psychopomps through the siege perilous, through the seven gates, until he is returned to the waiting arms of the Mother. He is lost in the underworlds, as often we are lost in the underworld. We must seek the wisdom of the oldest creatures. We must open the gates and provide safe passage for his rebirth.

We seek the Son of the Mother, within and without.
We seek the Light in the Heart of Darkness
We seek the Child stolen from the Mother and imprisoned in the Cold
We seek him as Mabon Ap Modron, As Pryderi, As Lugh, Gwyn, Taleisin and Lleu.
We seek him through the Ages of the World by the Wisdom of the Animal Teachers.

We start in the Center, with the Blackbird, Creature of the Fifth Age. Blackbird, tell us if you know of Mabon, the son of Modron, who was taken when three nights old from between his Mother and the wall?

Blackbird: *When first I came to this place, there was a blacksmith's anvil here. No work has been done on that anvil save by me sharpening my beak on it every night. There is not even a nut of that anvil left and in all that time I have never heard of Mabon, son of Modron. But I do know of one older than I and I will take you to him.*

To the North we travel, seeking out the Stag, Creature of the Fourth Age.

Stag, tell us if you know of Mabon, the son of Modron, who was taken when three nights old from between his Mother and the wall?

Stag: *When I first came to this place, there was only a single antler on each side of my head and no tree grew here save a single oak. That oak tree grew large and strong, with hundreds of branches. Long ago it fell and nothing is left but that stump and in all that time I have never heard of Mabon, son of Modron. But I do know of one older than I and I will take you to him.*

To the East we travel, seeking out the Owl, Creature of the Third Age.

Owl, tell us if you know of Mabon, the son of Modron, who was taken when three nights old from between his Mother and the wall?

Owl: *When I first came to this place, this great valley before us was a wooded glen. The race of man came and destroyed it. Then a second forest grew up. The forest here today is the third forest that has grown here. As for me, my wings have worn down to nothing but stump and in all that time I have never heard of Mabon, son of Modron. But I do know of one older than I and I will take you to him.*

To the South we travel, seeking out the Eagle, Creature of the Second Age.

Eagle, tell us if you know of Mabon, the son of Modron, who was taken when three nights old from between his Mother and the wall?

Eagle: *When I first came to this place long ago, I had a stone that I would stand on and peck at. Today, there is nothing left of the stone. In all that time I haven't heard of Mabon, son of Modron, except, when I went hunting for food in the lake. I sank my talons into large salmon, expecting to carry it off. Instead it dragged me down into the water and almost destroyed me. I went back with my relatives to destroy it, but it asked for peace and came to have tridents pulled out of its back. Unless the salmon knows something of Mabon, son of Modron, I know none that can help you.*

To the West we traveled, seeking out the Salmon, Creature of the First Age, Oldest of All Living Creatures. Salmon, tell us if you know of Mabon, the son of Modron, who was taken when three nights old from between his Mother and the wall?

Salmon: *I swim the streams between this world and that, to feed on the Hazelnuts of Wisdom. I have found the place where the Son of the Mother is hidden. The way is dangerous, through seven gates, through seven castles, amid many dangers and many treasures. If you would not believe me, ride with me there.*

Together, with the Creatures of the Great Ages as our allies, we descend to find Mabon. Travel as Arthur once did with his companions, seeking the otherworld treasures.

We descend together, spiraling downward, spiraling downward, spiraling downward.

We enter a dark descending tunnel, with only the light of our spirits to guide us.

By our sides are the blackbird, the stag, the owl, the eagle and the salmon, guiding us through the gates of the Underworld, of Annwn.

We approach the gate of the first castle, Caer Orchen,

the Castle of Dread, the Castle of Shelving Tide, Castle of the Sloping Sides.

This Castle of Dread is where we must divest ourselves of the body, of earthly concerns.

This Castle is our Root to all things Material, Sensual and Physical.

This Castle is where we open the gate to the Spirit World.

This Castle is where we release our attachments to the physical world and all its pleasures.

A guardian stops you at the gate, preventing you from passing.

How does the guardian appear? Is the guardian familiar, frightening or otherwise something you recognize as a key to help you master this gate?

You must make an offering to the guardian before you can pass.

What do you want to hold onto most from this life? Offer it to the guardian.

We approach the gate of the second castle, Caer Fandy-Manddwy,

the Castle on High, the Sea Castle, the Castle of Starry Prisons.

This Castle of the Sea is where we pass through the astral oceans.

This Castle is our Intimacy where we make connections to all life.

This Castle is where we learn to trust and immerse ourselves in the coming mystery.

A guardian stops you at the gate, preventing you from passing.

How does the guardian appear? Is the guardian familiar, frightening or otherwise something you recognize as a key to help you master this gate?

You must make an offering to the guardian before you can pass.

What prevents you from trusting yourself and trusting others? Offer it to the guardian.

We approach the gate of the third castle, Caer Goludd,

the Castle of Gloom, the Castle of Trials, the Castle of Death.

This Castle of Trials is where we learn the axis of Power and Fear.

This Castle is where we face our darkness.

This Castle is where we embrace our power and overcome the death of the self.

A guardian stops you at the gate, preventing you from passing.

How does the guardian appear? Is the guardian familiar, frightening or otherwise something you recognize as a key to help you master this gate?

You must make an offering to the guardian before you can pass.

What do you fear the most? Offer it to the guardian.

We approach the gate of the fourth castle, Caer Rigor,

the Castle of the Royal Horn, the Royal Castle.

This Castle of Royals is where we learn to love perfectly.

This Castle is where we find the Royal Heart loving all.

This Castle is where we seek harmony and balance.

A guardian stops you at the gate, preventing you from passing.

How does the guardian appear? Is the guardian familiar, frightening or otherwise something you recognize as a key to help you master this gate?

You must make an offering to the guardian before you can pass.

What stops you from loving all? Offer it to the guardian.

We approach the gate of the fifth castle, Caer Fredwyd,

the Castle of the Perfected Ones, Castle of Carousal, Castle of Revelry.

This Castle of Carousal is where we celebrate with the Mighty Dead who have gone before.

This Castle is where we open to the Voice of Wisdom from within and from the past.

This Castle is where we express that wisdom to all holy races of flesh and spirit.

A guardian stops you at the gate, preventing you from passing.

How does the guardian appear? Is the guardian familiar, frightening or otherwise something you recognize as a key to help you master this gate?

You must make an offering to the guardian before you can pass.

What stops you from hearing and speaking the wisdom of your ancestors?

Offer it to the guardian.

We approach the gate of the sixth castle, Caer Pedryfan,

the Revolving Castle, Four Cornered and Revolving Sky Castle,

The Four Squared Burial Castle.

This Castle of Revolving is where we see with True Sight.

This Castle is where we see all times, all places, all things.

This Castle is where we die and are reborn through our vision.

A guardian stops you at the gate, preventing you from passing.

How does the guardian appear? Is the guardian familiar, frightening or otherwise something you recognize as a key to help you master this gate?

You must make an offering to the guardian before you can pass.

What stops you from truly seeing all worlds as they are? Offer it to the guardian.

We approach the gate of the seventh castle, Caer Sidi,

the Castle of the Sidhe, Castle of the Zodiacal Wheel, Castle of the Inner Stars.

This Castle of Stars is where we began and where we shall end.

This Castle is where the Queen of the Starry Heavens resides.

This Castle is the Starry Kingdom in the Heart of the Underworld

where the Divine Fire resides.

A guardian stops you at the gate, preventing you from passing.

How does the guardian appear? Is the guardian familiar, frightening or otherwise something you recognize as a key to help you master this gate?

You must make an offering to the guardian before you can pass.

What stops you from finding the starry divinity within you? Offer it to the guardian.

Come into the Starry Castle.

You are greeted by She who is of the Silver Wheel.

She who Shapes Form from the Mist.

She who is Arianrhod, Starry Weaver.

She who is the Queen of the Castle.

The Queen of the Isle

The Lady of the Silvery Lake

The Keeper of the Apples of Immortality

Take this time to commune with the Silver Star Goddess.

As she is the Goddess of Silver Light,
She is also the Goddess of Darkness.
She is the Heart of the Underworld as well as being the light within its center.
She is paradox.
Receive the blessing of the Great Mother of Darkness,
As Modron, Ceridwen, Morrighan and Danu.

She reveals to you Mabon, Son of Modron, both within the Caer and within yourself.
See Mabon within and without
Feel Mabon within and without.
Know Mabon within and without.
Commune with the Child of Light, Hope and Promise.
Do whatever he asks to prepare his way and coming Rebirth at Yule.

When done, his light guides the way out of the seven gates, the seven castles.
Pass freely through the gate of seventh castle, Caer Sidi,
This Castle of Stars.
You are crowned by the Guardian who acknowledges your Sovereignty.

Pass freely through the gate of sixth castle, Caer Pedryfan,
This Revolving Castle of True Sight.
You are anointed with salve on your eyes and brow to see truly always.

Pass freely through the gate of the fifth castle, Caer Fredwyd,
This Castle of Carousal with the Wise and Mighty Dead.
You are given a torc or choker necklace to remember to always speak with wisdom.

Pass freely through the gate of the fourth castle, Caer Rigor,
This Castle of the Royal Heart.
You are given a medallion that hangs at your heart of Perfect Love.

Pass freely through the gate of the third castle, Caer Goludd,
This Gloomy Castle of Power and Fear.

You are given a golden bracelet, to shine and light your way.

Pass freely through the gate of the second castle, Caer Fandy-Manddwy,
This Sea Castle of Intimacy.
You are given a cord, your link to the first womb.

Pass freely through the gate of the first castle, Caer Orchen,
This Dread Castle of all things Material.
You are given a royal robe, concealing all these things yet granting power in the world.

Only Seven Returned from Caer Sidi.
No more. No less.
Only Seven Returned from Caer Sidi.
Seven within. Seven without.
Seven holy powers challenged and blessed, suffered and kissed.
Only Seven Returned from Caer Sidi.

Eat an apple, the fruit of the otherworld, in both celebration and to ground yourself after this intense journey. When ready, prepare to release your space by thanking the deities gathered.

We thank the Great Mother, the Goddess, the Source of Life
We thank Danu, Morrighan, Modron, Rhiannon, Arianrhod, Morgana
May there always be peace between us.
Stay if you will, go if you must.
Hail and farewell.

We thank the Great Father, the God, the Giver of Blessings
We thank Dagda, Nuada, Nudd, Pywll, Gwydion, Arthur
May there always be peace between us.
Stay if you will, go if you must.
Hail and farewell.

We thank the Child of Light within us all.
We thank the Child of Hope and Promise

Lugh, Mabon, Gwyn, Lleu, Pryderi
May there always be peace between us.
Stay if you will, go if you must.
Hail and farewell.

Release the quarters and the totemic teachers.

To the powers of the North, we thank and release the element of Earth and the Stag.
Hail and farewell.

To the powers of the West, we thank and release the element of Water and the Salmon.
Hail and farewell.

To the powers of the South, we thank and release the element of Air and the Eagle.
Hail and farewell.

To the powers of the East, we thank and release the element of Fire and the Owl.
Hail and farewell.

Complete the circle, returning to the North. Circle back to the front of the altar widdershins and acknowledge Spirit by saying:

And we thank Spirit, always with us, and the Blackbird. Hail and farewell.

Release the Circle as you cast it.

Much of this ritual draws upon similar mythic figures from other Celtic myths, not being purely about the Morrighan, or her aspect as the Avalonian Morgan. Yet the mythos of the seven-fold castle leads to the same place, the Faery otherworld in the depths of the Earth where light and darkness both rule supreme in paradox. The prose borrows liberally from translations of *The Mabinogion* as translated by Jeffery Gantz and *The Spoils of Annwn* as found in the book *Awen* by Mike Harris. The mystery teachings are a compilation found in the initiatory system of the Temple of Witchcraft, based upon the seven gates of the underworld as found in the Tale of Inanna. In the Temple, we compare that seven-fold system with the Caers of these myths, to the planets, alchemical stages, and the Traditional Craft teachings on the Miracle of Bread.

CHAPTER NINE
The heart of the Morrighan

The heart of the Morrighan, her essence, is found everywhere, though her work can be seen in three primary realms. She is the goddess of the living. Her living heart pumps with the blood of warriors and lovers and the heart of the green land, starting in Ireland and moving across the world. She is the Goddess of the Faeries. Her faery heart is the green beyond the grass of Ireland, the magickal emerald fire that lies below the land, where the Tuatha reside. Her faery heart is also the blue faery flame in the depths of this land, the blue of the waters of Avalon and its faery queen clad in the black of the depths and the white of the elder tree. She is the Goddess of the Dead. Her black heart is enshrouded by the phantom mist of the land of shades and apparitions. She is the darkness of the end and the whiteness of the bones of the ancestors.

Like a braid of three strands, they are stronger when woven together than when separated, but each individual thread must be understood and appreciated to work with the whole. Together the heart of this goddess is a triple rose that blooms in the wasteland, the rose that heals and redeems, bringing us into harmony with life, land and spirit.

THE POWER OF THE LIVING LAND

The blessings of the Morrighan embodied in the living land of the Great Between, the land of our Earth and all on it, are given to warriors and lovers and stewards of the land. The connecting thread between these three "classes" is the life force that flows through them. Each is connected by blood—the blood of the human life force pumping in all our veins, and the blood of the Earth—the streams, rivers and even the rivers of energy, the ley lines connecting the sacred sites. It is the flow that keeps all things alive. It is the flow regulated by the sacred heart that keeps us here in the world, be it the heart of flesh and blood or the heart of the land. All is one in the love of the Morrighan.

All warriors, lovers and stewards of the Earth are passionate about their lives. Each lives life to the fullest, experiencing triumphs to be celebrated and tragedies to be mourned. One cannot be a warrior without undergoing battle, within or without. Battles are won and lost, but the attitude with which one approaches the battles transforms the petty brawler into the spiritual warrior. Practitioners of every spiritual discipline at one time or another have been considered warriors. There is much in common between the knight, sorcerer and yogi. We learn from both sides of the cycle—win and lose.

The same can be said about the true lover. While today we think of love as an emotion or a state to attain and keep, it is in the giving and receiving, in the flow and process of relationship, where we truly are blessed with love. Sometimes we "win" and find a solid relationship, from lover to friends and family. Other times we don't, and we lose our love. The fragility of it makes it both precious and dangerous. Yet the love is its own reward.

Those who are in love with the land itself, ranging from goddess worshippers seeing the planet as the Great Mother, to those more academic environmentalists and simply lovers of nature, approach the land with both the intensity of the warrior, seeking to protect the Earth, and the tenderness of a lover and family member, truly cherishing the seeming fragility of the land. They learn to combine love and war with the land, and are thrice blessed by the Lady.

Rite for Sorcerous Power

While those embodying the flesh and blood aspects of the Morrighan's blessing might not conform to traditional ideas of sorcerers and Witches, the ability to create change in the world of shape and form on the surface of the Earth and in the realm of humanity, is magick. Magick is simply change. The Morrighan is the "source of all enchantments" and in the stories of the Tuatha, uses much of her power tactically, as a weapon. She creates changes on the battlefield. In some magickal traditions, the battlefield is a metaphor for life. Sorcerers in the Toltec traditions depicted by Carlos Castaneda are warrior-magicians. The battle to control, change and master the self is as much a part of their magick as is the battle to change outer conditions in the world. A wise occultist would say you cannot change the outer world until you first change the inner world. Occultist Dion Fortune's teachings on magick are based upon this concept.

Another metaphor for life and the "game" of battles in life is the chess or checkerboard. *Fidchell*, an ancient Irish game that is referenced in the mythologies and folktales and is compared to chess, is seen as a metaphor for the "game of life" by some Celtic-influenced Witches, including those of the Cabot Tradition of Witchcraft. Known as *gwyddbwyll* to the Welsh, traditionally it was reserved for Druids and nobles. It was said the board and pieces were magickally able to play themselves without human intervention. In many ways this is the typical human view of life, unfolding without our true active involvement. But warriors and magicians understood that they played the game, and could both be more actively engaged and somewhat detached, knowing it was a game, and that there was a larger, transhuman perspective to the game. The magick of the warrior-sorcerer is the active participation with the entire game board and pieces, rather than identifying solely with one piece on the board.

Dark goddesses such as the Morrighan in her many forms are considered tutelary in the magickal arts. While the myths have painted Morrighan more as the tutor of warriors through being a form of nemesis-teacher, I have found her quite educational in gaining magickal power and knowledge. But beware, for knowledge and power do not always equate with love and wisdom. She can teach many things, but how you use those things is up to you, and ultimately your responsibility. One need only to read her myths to know she has terrible things to show as well as wonderful things.

Set up an appropriate altar. Create sacred space by casting a circle. For the four quarters, invoke the four wizards of the fabled cities:

To the North, to the sacred city of Falias, I call to the realm of elemental earth.
I call upon the spirit of earth by the blessings of the wizard Morfesa,
Keeper of the Stone of Sovereignty.
Morfesa, teach me the ways of the Wort Cunner.
Show me the powers of the herbs and trees, the stones and the animals.
Teach me the ways of ice and stillness.
Hail and welcome.

To the East, to the sacred city of Gorias, I call to the realm of elemental air.
I call upon the spirit of air by the blessings of the wizard Esras,
Keeper of the Sword of Truth.
Esras, teach me the ways of the bard.
Show me the powers of the blade and shield, the tongue and the song.
Teach me the ways of story and art.
Hail and welcome.

To the South, to the sacred city of Finias, I call upon the element of fire.
I call upon the spirit of fire by the blessings of the wizard Uiscias,
Keeper of the Spear of Destiny.
Uiscias, teach me the ways of the smith.
Show me the powers of the hammer and anvil, the torch and the forge.
Teach me the ways of iron and blood.
Hail and welcome.

To the West, to the sacred city of Murias, I call upon the element of water.
I call upon the spirit of water by the blessings of the wizard Semias,
Keeper of the Cup of Compassion.
Semias, teach me the way of the Seer.
Show me the powers of the hand and the eye, the heart and the head.
Teach me the ways of the double and flight.
Hail and welcome.

Burn the Morrighan Incense. You could also use the Phantom Queen Incense or Morrighan Devotional Incense. Anoint yourself with the Morrighan Oil. Evoke the Morrighan to your ritual space and ask her to increase your "sorcerous power."

By She Who Is Three
I, (name yourself), call to thee.
Source of All Enchantments
Maker of Magick
Mother to Warriors, Witches and Guardians of the Land
I call to thee.
Increase my power. Increase my might. Increase my magick.
Open my Eye. Guide my Hand. Beat with my heart.
Grow within me the power,
As I am standing at the sacred center between the Four Fabled Cities
Where all secret knowledge is known and shared by the wizard poets.
Teach me all the magicks,
As I am standing at the sacred center between the Four Fabled Cities
Where all occult lore is known and shared by the wizard sages.
Bless me with the might,
As I am standing at the sacred center between the Four Fabled Cities
Where all sorcery is known and shared by the wizard kings.
So mote it be.

Make your offerings to the Morrighan. Use what you feel is most appropriate. I suggest a red wine infused with various non-toxic herbs of the Morrighan. You can pour it out into a chalice for her on the altar, or pour it out to the ground.

Enter into your trance state and envision yourself standing at the four-way crossroads. Approaching you from each of the four directions are the wizard kings of the fabled cities. Morfesa comes from the North. Esras comes from the East. Uiscias comes from the South and Semias comes from the West. How do you see each one? How do they approach you?

If they accept you in this working, each will mark you or bless you in some way. They might also each give you a gift of some sort, dealing with the arts they teach and embody. They might require a gift in return. If all four accept you in this working, a darkness will descend upon you, like a giant crow descending upon you, becoming like a crow cloak and headdress. You are covered in the black feathers. They surround you and interpenetrate you. They enter your body and energy, and each fills you with magickal power and might. They get within you and change you utterly.

When you are filled with as much as you can handle, the crow leaps upward again, leaving you with the blessing of the Morrighan. You can still feel the black feathers around you and in you, though they are now your own, not simply a cloak. You are remade through this power.

Thank the Morrighan and say your farewells. As the point of the ritual is to increase your power, do not "ground" the excess energy into the Earth, but imagine the energy grounding into the "earth" of your own bones, building your capacity to hold magickal power.

By She who is Three.
Great Morrighan
Source of Enchantment
Bestower of Power
I thank you.
I thank you.
I thank you.
May there always be peace between us.

When ready, release the four quarters.

To the North, to the sacred city of Falias,
I thank and release the powers of elemental earth
I thank and release the wizard Morfesa, keeper of the Stone of Sovereignty.
Thank you for opening the way of the Wort Cunner.
Hail and farewell.

To the West, to the sacred city of Murias,
I thank and release the powers of elemental water
I thank and release the wizard Semias, keeper of the Cup of Compassion.
Thank you for opening the way of the Seer.
Hail and farewell.

To the South, to the sacred city of Finias,
I thank and release the powers of elemental fire
I thank and release the wizard Uiscias, keeper of the Spear of Destiny.
Thank you for opening the way of the Smith.
Hail and farewell.

To the East, to the sacred city of Gorias,
I thank and release the powers of elemental air
I thank and release the wizard Esras, keeper of the Sword of Truth.
Thank you for opening the way of the Warrior.
Hail and farewell.

Then release the circle. If indoors, you can take your offerings outdoors to an appropriate spot and pour them out.

THE WORLD OF THE FAERY FOLK

If the heart of the Morrighan that is in the living land expresses all that is, here and now in the world of form, the World of the Faery folk embodies all that never was, in the world of the spirit. Here we have the elder race of spirit, yet those who are by their very nature not manifested in the world of form. They are tethered to the world of form, associated with nature, with plants, trees, rivers and stones, yet also apart from it, for their true home is dwelling in the depths and the land below. They exist in the light unseen by most mortal eyes. They are the people under the hills, residing where the Tuatha retreated with the coming of the current race of Irish people. Occultists can see their retreat as the metaphor for the chthonic powers retreating below planetary consciousness with the rise of human consciousness upon the world.

The flow of the Faery realm is one of the seasons, the tides of nature that rise and fall. In many ways, the tide rises up from the deep Earth, merging with the light of the Sun, Moon and stars, only to descend again to its point of origin, the deep Earth where the heart of the mother resides. The high fey are the priestesses and priests ministering to the tides of both our worlds. It is said that in the realms beyond the mortal world, things are in mirror opposition. Day is night. Night is day. Summer is winter and fall is spring. Described in the Voodou traditions as the mirror fantastic, to the Celtic faery seer, this is the glassy still surface of the lake, perfectly reflecting the world below. It is the gate and the portal to the mysteries of the faery and their enchantment.

There is a reciprocal nature between the world of form and the world of Faery, as there is a partnership between these priestly fey and the Witches and wizards, the Druids and seers of old. Together, we harness the flow from above to below and below to above, to turn the Wheel of the Year and keep balance in all worlds. Like the scales of Justice, like the goddess of Egypt with many faces but embracing the balance of Ma'at, the Morrighan manifests to do what is necessary to keep balance, and at heart, that is root to many of her most mysterious acts of violence and seduction. She, like the Fey, is beyond human, and does what is necessary, not what is personal, to maintain the balance.

Those who work with the fey folk in the capacity of necessity are blessed, but seem to stand ever apart from those who operate from a place of sentiment and personality. The personally oriented do as they want to satisfy their own internal dialogues and motivations, and the concept of necessity for a higher purpose eludes them. Those who stand apart find shelter in the faery heart of the Morrighan.

Rite of Prophecy

Those embraced by the elder faery race are renowned for many skills—artistry and music, magick and healing, but they are often best known for their seership—the power to see things as they truly are, were and will be. Many touched with faery blood and blessings have the "sight" and see and know things before they will occur. While Neopagans actively engage the development of psychic abilities as part of the magician's training, those with natural gifts of psychic sight in the Celtic traditions don't often see it as a blessing. It is as much a burden and responsibility as an asset. The Morrighan, as Faery Queen, is a prophet. After the battle with the Fomorians, she prophesizes the future and then the end of the world. She has the ability to confer her sight and her visions to others who work with her. Some gain them naturally, and some seek them out.

Set up an appropriate space and ambiance for the ritual. Use anything you feel both increases psychic power and connects you to the faery realm. Cast a circle and create your sacred space in whatever way is appropriate for you.

Burn Morrighan Prophetic Incense or Morgana the Faery Queen Incense. Use the Faery Queen Oil or simply the basic Morrighan Oil. Place the oil specifically on your brow, and where the skull and spine meet behind your head. Evoke the Morrighan as Seer and Faery Queen into your ritual space:

By She Who Is Three
I, (name yourself), call to thee.
Speaker of the Prophecy
Seer of the Past
Seer of the Present
Seer of the Future

I call to thee.
Queen of the Sidhe (She)
Queen of Faery
Queen of the Good Folk of the Hollow Hills
I call to thee
Open my eyes to the sight of the true
Open my eyes in a manner that is correct and good
Open my skills as the seers, to perceive that which was, is and will be
For the good of myself
For the good of my people
For the good of the world.
So mote it be.

Make your offerings to the Morrighan. Appropriate Faery Queen offerings are whiskey or scotch, white wine, bread, cake, milk, cheese, cream and honey. Enter your trance state through meditative vision.

From the four corners of the circle, from the Four Fabled Cities beyond, feel a troop of beings approaching, four troops in all. From each direction, from each world, they march. Some might be elementally influenced, embodying traits of earth, air, fire and water, like the medieval alchemists' image of elemental faeries—gnomes, sylphs, drakes and undines. But as the troops continue, the smaller elemental spirits give way to larger and more powerful, and more balanced beings from nature. Gathering towards you are the trooping faeries, the good folk from beyond the veil.

The spirits of deep nature reach you and surround you, circling you in rings moving clockwise and counterclockwise. From the directions of fire, water and air are three faery queens, clad in red, blue and yellow. and from the direction of earth, a king burning with black flame, crowned with the horns of a stag.

The circle parts to allow the royals of the troop access to you.

The three queens each touch your brow with their red, blue and yellow light. Each blazes upon your brow. Each awakens a different psychic perspective in you. The lights allow you to see, to hear and to know more clearly than ever before. The lights descend from the brow into the heart, bestowing that same seeing, hearing and knowing from the heart space, and then descend again into the belly, allowing the belly to see, hear and know from the place of body wisdom.

The three ladies become one and assume the familiar form of the Morrighan, but as Faery Queen. The lights within you become one, and your sense of perception is strengthened and heightened.

The king comes forward, and places upon your head a crown of antlers and black flame, extending your powers.

At this time the various faery guides may speak to you and guide you. Take this time to commune.

Thank all those who have gathered with you and return from your trance state. Feel the psychic eye awakened within you. Say your farewells to the Morrighan:

By She who is Three.
Great Morrighan
Faery Queen
Giver of Sight
I thank you.
I thank you.
I thank you.
May there always be peace between us.

Release the sacred space in a manner appropriate to the way you created it. Ground and balance. Make sure the offerings are properly left in nature for the Good Folk and their Queen.

THE ANCESTRAL REALM

Here we have the hidden heart of the goddess, the land of the dead. While celebrated as a goddess of battle, her aspect as the Phantom Queen is overlooked, yet here we focus upon it. Here is the heart of what was, or rather of who was. Here she is queen of those who were, those remembered and forgotten and those trapped between as shades, specters and phantoms. The line between Faery and ghost is blurry, as both are incorporeal and in times past, a difference was not recognized. Is the Bean Sidhe, or Banshee, a faery warning, or haunting ghost? Could it not be both? To those times and cultures that deified their dead, when the dead are returned to the land, they are living with the faery folk under the hills. Here within the land they can grow wise. The line between the faery races and the ancestors are blurry indeed, and the line between faeries and gods is equally blurry.

As queen of phantoms, specters and shades, she is also queen of the wandering dead, the restless and hungry ghosts who wander the worlds. She is the goddess of the seen and unseen, the living and the dead. In many ways, she is the goddess of the journey, in her horse aspect, like a psychopomp, leading souls from one destination to another. While she has not traditionally figured into the European image of the Wild Hunt near Samhain, as other European figures such as Odin/Wotan, Holda and Diana, through her natural functions, she could very well be a leader of such a procession of souls, gathering up the shades and ghosts from the year and returning them to the world of spirit to await rebirth, or she is the otherworldly queen the procession returns to at the end of their journey.

The question of ghosts, ancestors and reincarnation has always played upon my mind when comparing modern metaphysics and new lore with Celtic traditions. We are told from Caesar that the Celts believed in reincarnation, as they did in the mystery schools of Greece, for the Druids taught the Celtic warriors this doctrine to make them fearless in battle. Yet due to cultural context, we believe the Celts didn't have a global view of reincarnation and karma. To die a Celtic warrior would hold the promise of being reborn within the bloodlines and tribes, and not necessarily to be reborn in the next life as a Roman or Egyptian. Perhaps the reincarnation of the Celt was through genetic memory, and not necessarily the transmigration of the soul, or perhaps they were the same phenomenon. Yet in our modern era, we have past-life recall experiences that span the globe, where a Caucasian can have memories of lives in Asia, Egypt, Africa and India, without an obvious blood tie. And when we revere the ancestors, and they answer, how can they if they are on a path to reincarnation?

While I think no one metaphysical model is the absolute truth, one view has tended to dominate my view and relates very strongly to the triple nature of the Morrighan. I look for models that tend to validate multiple points of view as true, while still giving views and techniques that are helpful and direct. The model of the three souls has provided the greatest wisdom for me regarding the nature of reincarnation.

The basic three-souls concept is found in many magickal traditions, and made its way into Neopaganism and Witchcraft strangely through the Hawaiian teachings of Max Freedom Long, but parallels are found in Egypt, Hebrew and Siberia. The concept has become part of teachings of the Anderson Feri Tradition, the Reclaiming Tradition and in my own teachings in the Temple of Witchcraft.

The core of the three-soul model states we have not a body and a soul, but at least three distinct souls, or parts of our consciousness. We have a higher soul, a lower soul and a middle soul. The higher soul is what most traditions think of as the perfected individual consciousness, existing fundamentally beyond time and space. It is described as a "soul bird" and in my own work with the Morrighan, I see it as a "soul crow," but other traditions describe it as a dove or hawk. This is also known as the Holy Guardian Angel or Bornless One in ceremonial magick traditions. The middle soul is the personality, the ego and the sense of self in the world. This relates to the body and especially the face, the human self-identity. The lower soul is the double, equated with the astral body. It is intuitive, childlike and almost animalistic. Some refer to it as the fetch or fetch beast because of these non-verbal qualities. The work of magick is to align these souls into one unit.

Upon death, some teach that the three souls of an unenlightened, unaligned individual will separate. The higher soul ascends like a bird into the branches of the great world tree to await rebirth. The choices of the higher soul are global. The next life might be anywhere. The lower soul descends and returns to the underworld. It fills the pools of ancestral wisdom, and will rise up from the whole when another of the same "tribe" conceives a child. The middle soul most often stays with the body, and fades as the body decomposes. Traditions of cremation hasten this process so nothing keeps the higher and lower souls bound together and they can both continue their journey. Strong middle souls become guardians and household spirits if fed properly or find an alternative "food" source of spiritual energy. Those who die in a restless state, or with extreme violence, become the ghosts, shades and phantoms of the middle world—wandering with the personality, memories and emotions of the individual, but not exactly their full divine essence.

When you commune with the dead, or get memories from past lives into your conscious self, you are working with one of these three selves. Each contains the holographic potential, the entirety of the individual in life. When you connect to the higher self, you communicate with all of the individual, though the experience is somewhat detached. Even when the higher soul connects to a new incarnation, part of it is always outside of space and time. Tribal traditions that feed ancestors in return for blessings from the ancestors are most likely working through the tribal connections of the lower soul. The lower soul has more power, but tends to be more "hungry" to effect change, so it must be given offerings and attention. The middle soul is found in graveyards typically, and its energy seeps into the land. Graveyard dirt can therefore be used for magick. It contains the power and virtues of the deceased's Earthly vocation. Graveyards can also be connections to the other souls as well. The Celtic tradition of head hunting and the use of skulls is a method to retain the middle soul's power and knowledge, or to create a touchstone to the lower or higher self for prophecy and divination.

In a Celtic text known as *The Cauldron of Posey,* three "cauldrons" in the body are described, leading some to think they are like the chakra "wheels" of the Hindus, but in a more simplified and poetic form. Various modern interpretations exist on these cauldron centers. I refer to the lower cauldron as the Cauldron of Life, as it deals with the functioning of the body and the primal self. The lower soul corresponds with it. The middle center is the Cauldron of the Heart, and works with the human self. The head involves the Cauldron of Inspiration, and when in proper working order, the flow of Awen, of inspiration and poetic magick. It is the center of the Higher Self.

The Morrighan, also triune in nature, is Queen of all these souls. She is the crow goddess in the branches of the trees watching with the higher souls. She is the horse goddess, gathering up the souls of the middle world who haunt and wander. She is the cow that feeds the body and the wolf who teaches the tribe. She is the eel of the dark waters, the pools of the lower soul's ancestral blood. She can aid in you working with all of the dead. She can open the way to direct communication.

Soul Alignment

Breathe deeply. Breathe out all that doesn't serve. Breathe in the life force that is carried upon the breath, what the Hindu traditions refer to as prana and the Hebrew traditions refer to as ruach. Many equate the Welsh term awen with these words, though awen is life force and so much more, the divine drops of inspiration, for without life force, one will not be inspired. Notice there are three parts to your lungs, the abdominal lower portion, the thoracic middle portion and the upper clavicular area. With a full deep breath, they are like a balloon, filling the bottom, middle and top when you inhale, and releasing from the top, middle and bottom when you exhale. Take a moment to make sure you are breathing from all three sections of your lungs.

When ready, breathe deeply and imagine that your heart is like a mouth, on the sternum. A second mouth is in the center of your back. As you breathe, these two mouths are drawing in the energy of this life force into the heart area. While the heart is the nexus where all three souls can co-join, it is the middle of our three cauldrons where the middle self is found. As you breathe, you might align with the Morrighan's totems of the middle world, the horse, the wolf and the cow perhaps. In the Temple of Witchcraft, we call this self the Namer, for it likes to name, identify, label and organize things. It also likes to name and label emotions, relationships and people. While naming can be a handy skill, the Namer creates problems when unbalanced, or when it does not recognize the other selves.

When the heart center is energized, breathe in and through the souls of your feet. Draw the breath energy up to the belly. Fill the belly cauldron with this life force. This restores the vitality of your body and attunes to your primal self. You might be reminded of the most primal of the Morrighan's totems, the eel, or perhaps another serpent-like creature. In the Temple of Witchcraft, we refer to this self as the Shaper, as it likes to play and give things shape and form with its intention and emotions. It likes color, texture and all the senses.

When the belly center is energized, breathe in through the crown of the head. Draw the energy into the crown. Fill the crown. You might feel the presence of the crow or raven as the soul bird, the Watcher as it is known in the Temple of Witchcraft. Watchers are another association with angels, a nod to the Holy Guardian Angel name for this soul.

When the head center is energized, breathe in from all three zones at once. Draw them together so they mingle at the heart. Feel them come into alignment and balance at the heart. Find your center in the heart. Through the heart the higher self and lower self can best be expressed in your human life.

The words used in the Temple Soul Alignment with these breaths are:

I am the Namer
I am the Shaper
I am the Watcher
I am the Three in One
The One in Three
As it was, as it is, as it always shall be.
Blessed be.

Keep breathing with this awareness. The ritual does not need to be closed or grounded, as you hope to keep this alignment in your daily life. You can do it prior to any meditation or ritual work.

Samhain Ritual

Of all the holidays, Samhain is the one most closely associated with the Morrighan, and most closely associated in Paganism with the festivals of the dead. It is a time to honor the ancestors and ask for advice and aid, often in the form of divination. Shamanic journey is also appropriate to have direct contact with the gods. The Dagda, seeking the advice and blessing of the

Morrighan on the eve of Samhain before the Tuatha's battle with the Fomorians is a great example of this tradition. Even the Great God Dagda seeks her counsel.

Set an appropriate altar for Samhain. Traditional Wiccan colors are the colors of Halloween, black and orange. Use fruits and vegetables of the season, such as apples and gourds. While pomegranates are not a part of Celtic traditions, they have certainly become staples for Neopagan Samhains, and I like to include them. Skull fetishes, in form of stone-carved skulls or wax candles are also appropriate. Photos of loved ones from your ancestral altar are also appropriate in this rite. Burn Morrighan Phantom Queen incense or Prophecy Incense. Have the Morrighan Oil in a bottle and the Morrighan Elixir in the altar chalice or horn. Also have a black cloak or a black shawl or blanket for this rite. It is also helpful to have an oraclular device upon the altar. While tarot cards and runes are most popular, the ogham sticks are more culturally appropriate.

Align the three souls. Cast circle to create your sacred space. Use quarter calls you feel are appropriate, or try these totem quarter calls.

To the North
I call upon the element of Earth.
I call upon the great Cow, provider of milk and nourishment.
Please bless us with your guidance and protection.
Hail and welcome

To the East
I call upon the element of Fire
I call upon the powerful Wolf, provider of teachings.
Please bless us with your guidance and protection.
Hail and welcome.

To the South
I call upon the element of Air.
I call upon the wise Crow, keeper of sacred law.
Please bless us with your guidance and protection.
Hail and welcome.

To the West
I call upon the element of Water.

I call upon the primal Eel, master of shapeshifting.
Please bless us with your guidance and protection.
Hail and welcome.

Stoke your incense. Anoint yourself with oil. Petition the awareness of the Morrighan on this night.

By She Who Is Three
I, (name yourself), call to thee.
Mysterious One at the river's edge,
I call to thee.
Giver of counsel, mistress of strategy,
I call to thee.
Blessed with blood, defeating my enemies,
I call to thee.
Queen of Spirits and Specters,
Queen of Sidhe and Sith
Queen of Phantoms and Ancestors
I call to thee.
Queen of the Company,
Queen of the Order
Sovereign of the Mighty Dead,
On this Samhain night when the veil is thin
Please be here now!

Light three candles for the Morrighan, in the "traditional" goddess colors of white, red and black.

Make any appropriate offerings of food, candy, coffee, alcohol, tobacco and other smokes, sweets or rich food for both the dead and the Morrighan. You can light candles to the dead you specifically want to communicate with in this ritual. Name them. Invite them to the circle. By the grace of the Morrighan, Queen of the Dead, they shall pass and you will be safe.

Make a sacrament of the Morrighan elixir. As you drink, feel the magick of the herbs within it.

Once you feel sufficiently prepared, enter an ecstatic trance by using the edges of your cloak or shawl like wings. Holding the ends in your hands, flap them like wings. I tend to spin around as I do it, getting both a dizzy high and becoming tired, until I gently lower myself down onto the ground. Assume the "hanged man" pose from the tarot. I prefer the right leg raised and crossed over a vertical straight left leg, with the hands either behind the back as in the Rider-Waite Tarot, or outstretched over the head, as the Hanged Man trump from the Thoth deck of Aleister Crowley and Lady Freda Harris.

Hanged Man Pose

This position will facilitate a powerful trance to reach the goddess. You will find her at a liminal place—the river, an island shore, the crossroads or the gallows. Speak to her. She may guide loved ones who have passed to you at this time. She may guide ancestors of blood and spirit from ages past. She can even join you with the Mighty Dead, the masters of the craft from all times and lands. You will be guided by her dark hand.

The experience will draw to a completion. Rise up from your underworld threshold and rise up in flesh and blood off the ground. Make your offering and libations to the goddess and the spirits. Ask for an omen and draw one to three from your oraclular device. Ask for guidance in correct interpretation and then gaze at the omens chosen. Interpret them to the best of your ability, and if needed, later consult a guide, expert or even a book.

When done, thank the Great Goddess.

Sovereign of the Dead and Mighty Dead
Queen of Phantoms above, below and between
I thank you.
Hail and farewell.

Thank the spirits of the dead and any and all who might have joined you. Bless them in love and trust. Then release the quarters.

To the North
I thank and release the element of Earth.
I thank and release the great Cow.
Thank you for your guidance and protection.
Thank you for your nourishment.
Hail and farewell.

To the West
I thank and release the element of Water.
I thank and release the primal Eel.
Thank you for your guidance and protection.
Thank you for your shapeshifting.
Hail and farewell.

To the South
I thank and release the element of Air.
I thank and release the wise Crow.
Thank you for your guidance and protection.
Thank you for your sacred law.
Hail and farewell.

To the East
I thank and release the element of Fire.

I thank and release the powerful Wolf.
Thank you for your guidance and protection.
Thank you for your teachings.
Hail and farewell.

Release the circle in the customary manner. Make appropriate use of the offerings that remain, taking those that can be released into the Earth into nature.

CONCLUSION
The Feast Is Prepared

The Feast of the Morrighan, while a collection of history, myth, poetry, ritual and magick, is really a call to celebrate this magnificent and often misunderstood power in the world. The table is set with both death, as often popularized by this war goddess, and life, for she is one of sensuality, sexuality and the land. All things that sustain us are ultimately sustained by the underworld, the darkness. The seeds grow in darkness and come out into the light, whispering their sweet secrets from the depths and providing us with a nourishment on many levels.

The Feast of the Morrighan can refer to the Feast of Tara, or the Great Assembly of Tara, the *Feis Teamhrach*. Established by King Ollamh Fodhla, there are quite a few conflicting theories on it, ranging from the rites of kingship held near Samhain over the course of seven days for religious purposes, to rites of civil order and law. Similar gatherings might have taken place on a smaller scale at Emain Macha. These are parallels to the assemblies held at the opposite point of the year, Beltane, considered a festival of life and sexuality by today's Neopagans. Together, they are celebrations of light and dark, life and death. The Morrighan, in all her rich guises, is an embodiment of the wheel of transformation, the life from death and the death from life, eternally entwined in many feminine faces and points in history.

To truly live fully in the world, we must embrace both. Those who face the ordeal of true initiation do so, facing death and living with it as an ally. The Morrighan is such an ally, informing us of the blessings of life through its fragility and the eternal possibility of death. We live fully in the world by honoring her, and the goddess in her most primal form, through the Earth, nature and all women everywhere.

QUARTER CALLS FOR THE FIVE PROVINCES OF IRELAND

CALLS

To the North, to the land of Ulster,
The land of Macha where the warrior's fire burns strong
Please bring the blessing of the warrior—courage and strength
Hail and welcome.

To the East, to the land of Leinster
The land of Brigit where the lady's mantle is ever green
Please bring the blessings of prosperity—abundance and health
Hail and welcome.

To the South, to the land of Munster
The land of the Cailleach where the crone's water rises
Please bring the blessings of the artist—creativity and inspiration
Hail and welcome

To the West, to the land of Connacht
The land of Medb where the winds blow strong
Please bring the blessings of the scholar—magick and eloquence
Hail and welcome.

To the Center, to the land of the Meath
The land of Ériu
Please bring the blessings of Tara—Stewardship and Sacredness
Hail and welcome.

RELEASES

To the Center, to the land of the Meath
The land of Ériu, the lady of the Emerald Isle
We thank you for the blessings of Tara—Stewardship and Sacredness
Hail and farewell.

To the North, to the land of Ulster,
The land of Macha where the warrior's fire burns strong
We thank you for the blessing of the warrior—courage and strength.
Hail and farewell.

To the West, to the land of Connacht
The land of Medb where the winds blow strong
We thank you for the blessings of the scholar—magick and eloquence
Hail and farewell.

To the South, to the land of Munster
The land of the Cailleach where the crone's water rises
We thank you for the blessings of the artist—creativity and inspiration
Hail and farewell

To the East, to the land of Leinster
The land of Brigit where the lady's mantle is ever green
We thank you for the blessings of prosperity—abundance and health
Hail and farewell.

Glossary

Aed Ruad: Father of Macha Mongruad. King of Ireland.

Aengus: Tuatha De Dannan god of love and beauty.

Alchemy: The study of inner and outer transmutation, most often associated with Hermeticism.

Anu: Another name for Danu. Sometimes one of the three goddesses of the Morrighan. Also named Annan

Ard Mhacha: Macha's High Place also called Armagh.

Badb: Crow or Badb Catha, Battle Crow. One of the goddesses most frequently associated with the Morrighan.

Balor: Fomorian leader known for his evil eye and battle with Lugh.

Banba: One of the infrequently mentioned goddesses included in the Morrighan or Morrigu. Sister to Ériu and Fódla. Together the embody Ireland.

Bellona: Roman war goddess associated with Mars, either as his wife, sister or daughter.

Bodhran: A Celtic drum that uses a double headed beater.

Brian: Considered to be one of the three sons of Danu, and the Morrighan, along with Luchar and Lucharba.

Celtic Reconstructionism: A movement to reconstruct traditions from Celtic cultures based upon proven historic source material rather than a reliance on occult or Neopagan traditions.

Cimbaeth: Cousin of Aed Ruad and husband of Macha Mongruad. King of Ireland.

Crunnchu: Husband of the fourth Macha, who bragged of his wife's speed and magick such that she was forced to run against horses while pregnant.

Dagda: The "Good God" of the Irish pantheon of the Tuatha de Dannan. A giant who possesses a magick club that can bring death and life, a harp that changes the season and a cauldron that is never empty of food. A lover of the Morrighan.

Delbaeth: Father of Badb. Also father of Ériu, Banba and Fodla.

Dithorba: Cousin of Aed Ruad. Killed by Macha Mongruad. King of Ireland.

Elcmar: Son of Delbaeth and father of Nemain.

Emain Macha: Macha's Neckbrooch. A fortress created by Macha Mongruad.

Erinyes: Furies, or Angry Ones. Goddesses of justice and revenge in Greek myth.

Ériu: The Goddess of Ireland, from which it gets its name. Along with Fódla and Bamba, the three goddesses considered to embody Ireland.

Ernmas: Witch goddess and mother of the Morrighan, Danu, Ériu, Fódla and Banba. Her name means Iron Death.

Ethniu: Daughter of Balor. Mother of Lugh and Delbaeth.

Eumenides: The new name of the Erinyes, renamed the Kindly Ones to appease their fury.

Fea: Nemain's sister.

Fir Bolgs: A race that inhabits Ireland prior to the invasion of the Tuatha de Dannan. Often considered monsters or forces of chaos.

First Battle of Moytura: Battle between the Fir Bolgs and the Tuatha de Dannan for control of Ireland.

Fódla: One of the sisters of Ériu. Along with Fódla, the three goddesses considered to embody Ireland.

Formorian: An elder race of sea faring beings who inhabited Ireland prior to the Fir Bolgs, Tuatha de Dannan and Milesians (Irish).

Fortune, Dion: British occultist, author and often unacknowledged influence on modern Paganism and Witchcraft. Famous for her work fusing Pagan, Hermetic and Christian elements into a harmonious occult practice, as well as for her novels, particularly *The Sea Priestess*.

Freya: Norse goddess associated with love, sex and witchcraft. Considered a Venusian archetype by occult traditions.

Gliten: One of the nine sisters of Avalon.

Gliton: One of the nine sisters of Avalon.

Glitonea: One of the nine sisters of Avalon.

Hecate: Greek underworld goddess triple in nature and considered the Queen of Witches. Often depicted as a crone in modern lore, but perceived as a torch bearing maiden in ancient lore.

Hermes: Greek god of communication, commerce and thieves. Also a psychopomp.

Hermeticism: Philosophical and magickal studies associated with master teacher Hermes Trismegestus, or Triple Great Hermes. Sometimes equated with the Greek god Hermes, the messenger and psychopomp.

Imram: Voyage, often referring to a psychic or spirit journey.

Isis: Most popular Egyptian Goddess. Sister and wife to Osiris. Often considered by occultists to be Mother Nature or the Great Goddess.

Janus: Two-faced Roman God. One face looks to the future while the other behind to the past. Thresholds and doorways are sacred to him.

King Conchobar mac Nessa: A king of Ulster who forces Macha to run while pregnant, to beat his horses and save the life of her husband Crunnchu, who bragged of her.

Lilith: Adam's first wife in esoteric Judaism. Considered a mother of demons and often called the Witch Mother in certain Gnostic Witchcraft traditions.

Luchar: Considered to be one of the three sons of Danu, and the Morrighan, along with Brian and Lucharba.

Lucharba: Considered to be one of the three sons of Danu, and the Morrighan, along with Brian and Luchar.

Ma'at: Egyptian goddess who embodied cosmic balance and harmony.

Macha: An aspect of the Morrighan associated with horses, crows, the land, faeries, twins, queens and curses. Also Mhacha.

Macha Mongruad: Macha of the Red Tresses. The most historic of the Machas.

Matronna: Gaulish mother goddess often connected with Danu, Don and Modron.

Mazoe: One of the nine sisters of Avalon.

Medusa: Greek mythological figure with snakes for hair and her gaze can turn people to stone.

Mercury: Roman god of communication, commerce and thieves as well as a psychopomp. Equated with Hermes of the Greeks.

Modron: Welsh Mother Goddess, often equated with Don and Danu.

Morgan: Welsh/Arthurian Lady of the Lake. Usually referencing the sea in her name.

Morgan Le Fey: Transformation of Morgan into faery villain in the Arthurian stories.

Morrighan: The Phantom Queen or Great Queen of the Irish Celtic Tradition. The spelling Morrighan, with an "h" refers to the collective goddess entity, much like term Morrigu, separate from the spelling Morrigan, used in this text to refer to an individual deity appearing alongside other aspects of the greater collective goddess.

Moronoe: One of the nine sisters of Avalon.

Morrighan: Often synonymous with Morrigan and Morgan. For the purposes of this text, Morrighan, with an "h," refers to the collective and all encompassing goddess while Morrigan refers to historical passages where Morrigan appears to refer to a single individual appearing alongside other aspects of the collective goddess, such as Badb and Macha in a narrative.

Neit: Husband of both Badb and Nemain.

Nemain: One of the goddesses most frequently associated with the Morrighan. Also spelled Nemon. She is known for her shrieking and her name means frenzy or panic.

Nemed: Husband of the second Macha.

Nemesis: Greek goddess of justice and retribution.

Nephthys: Dark sister to Isis, Osiris and Set. Wife of Set and mother of Anubus.

Neptur: Fomorian who killed Nemain and Badb.

Ogma: Tuatha de Dannan god of poetry, eloquence and battle. Often equated with Hercules of the Greeks. The alphabet Ogham is said to get its name from this god.

Partholon: Father of the First Macha.

Polytheistic: Belief in many gods. Hard polytheists believe in the absolute separation of individual gods. Soft polytheists believe in an inherent oneness between the gods, and possibly all things. Soft polytheism is common in Hermetic and other occult traditions.

Ragnarok: Norse concept of the apocalypse, or end of the world and start of a new one.

Reiki: A Japanese hands on and distant healing tradition passed via attunement (initiation). Practitioners have the ability to channel pure life force, ki, to facilitate healing without taking on illness or harm from their client.

Thiten: One of the nine sisters of Avalon.

Thiten cithara notissima: Also Thetis. One of the nine sisters of Avalon.

Tisiphone: One of the three furies, meaning avenging murder.

Tuan: Survivor of the first settlement of Ireland, who lives to tell the tale of Partholon and the first Macha.

Tyronoe: One of the nine sisters of Avalon.

Weaver Goddess: A manifestation of the creator Goddess as weaver of fate, time and space. Often perceived as a spider or as the three fates found in many forms of Indo-European mythology.

bibliography

Anderson, Leigh-Ann. *The Mythology of Ancient Ireland — The Five Waves of Invasion. http://www.suite101.com/content/the-mythology-of-ancient-ireland--the-five-waves-of-invasion-a324405:* Dec 23, 2010.

Andrews, Ted. *Animal-Speak: the Spiritual & Magical Powers of Creatures Great and Small.* Lewellyn Publications, St. Paul, MN, 1993.

Bendis. *The Blue Robuck: Morrighu. http://www.blueroebuck.com/morrighu.html:* September 3, 2010.

Blamires, Steve. *The Little Book of the Great Enchantment.* R.J. Stewart Books: 2008.

Cabot, Laurie with Jean Mills. *Celebrate the Earth: A Year of Holidays in the Pagan Tradition.* Dell Publishing, New York, 1994.

Conway, D.J. *The Ancient & Shining Ones.* Llewellyn Publications, St. Paul, Minnesota, 1993.

Corrigan, Ian. *Celtic Sorcery: A Druids Grimoire.* Starwood Edition, 2005.

Corrigan, Ian. *The Portal Book: Teachings and Works of Celtic Witchcraft.* The Association of Consciousness Exploration, Cleveland, Ohio, 1996.

Cowan, Tom. *Fire in the Head.* Harper San Francisco, New York, New York: 1993.

Epstein, Angelique Gulermovich. *War Goddess: The Morrígan and her Germano-Celtic Counterparts.* Doctor of Philosophy in Folklore and Mythology. University of California, Los Angeles, 1998.

Farrar, Stewart and Janet. *The Witches' Goddess: The Feminine Principle of Divinity.* Phoenix Pubishing, WA: 1987.

Fries. Jan. *Cauldron of the Gods: A Manual of Celtic Magick.* Mandrake Press. Oxford, UK: 2003.

Gore, Belinda. *Ecstatic Body Postures: An Alternative Reality Workbook.* Bear & Company, Santa Fe, NM: 1995.

Guiley, Rosemary Ellen. *The Encyclopedia of Witches & Witchcraft.* Checkmark Books, New York, New York, 1999.

Harris, Mike. *Awen: The Quest of the Celtic Mysteries.* Foreword by Gareth Knight. Oceanside, CA: Sun Chalice Books, 1999.

Hennessey, W.M. *The Ancient Irish Goddess of War.* 1870. *www.sacred-texts.com:* August 12, 2010.

Hunt, Augustus. *The Secrets of Avalon: An Introduction to Arthurian Druidism.* Avalonia, UK: 2010.

Jones, Kathy. *Priestess of Avalon Priestess of the Goddess.* Ariadne Publication: Somerset, UK: 2006.

Keating, Geoffrey. *The History of Ireland (BOOK I-II)* *http://www.ucc.ie/celt/published/T100054/index.html:* August 12.

Knight, Gareth, *The Secret Tradition of the Arthurian Legend.* Weiser Books, York Beach, ME, 1996.

Laurie, Erynn Rowan. 1996. *The Cauldron of Poesy.* Madstone Press. *http://www.thunderpaw.com/neocelt/poesy.htm:* May 2010.

Macleod, Fiona. *The Divine Adventure.* University of Michigan: 2009.

Matthews, John. *The Celtic Shaman: A Handbook.* Element, Inc., Rockport, MA: 1992.

Matthews, John. *Celtic Totem Animals: Meeting your animal helpers on your own shamanic journey.* Red Wheel/Weiser, Boston MA: 2002.

Matthews, Caitlin and John. *Encyclopedia of Celtic Wisdom.* New York: Barnes & Noble, 1996.

Monaghan, Patricia. *The Red-Haired Girl from the Bog: The Landscape of Celtic Myth and Spirit.* New World Library: 2004.

Monaghan, Patricia. *The Encyclopedia of Celtic Mythology and Folklore.* Checkmark Books: 2008.

National Museums Northern Ireland. *The Flora of Northern Ireland.* *http://www.habitas.org.uk/flora/splist.asp:* August 24, 2010.

Nichmacha, Sharynne MacLeod. *Queen of the Night: Rediscovering the Celtic Moon Goddess.* Weiser Books, Boston, MA: 2005.

Rankine, David and Sorita d'Este. *The Guises of the Morrigan.* Avalonia, UK: 2005.

Sjoestedt, Marie-Louise. *Celtic Gods and Heroes.* Dover Publications: 2008.

Valiente, Doreen. *An ABC of Witchcraft Past and Present.* St. Martin's Press, Inc. New York, New York; 1973.

Valiente, Doreen. *The Rebirth of Witchcraft.* Robert Hale: 2008.

OTHER ONLINE RESOURCES

http://earthenblacksmith.tripod.com/id43.html: August 24, 2010

http://kompost.ingreid.se/forum/viewtopic.php?
f=80&t=83&p=783&sid=ab0d0ecf53bf433b380319ee1ef56aae: August 12, 2010

http://www.sacred-texts.com/neu/cmt/cmteng.htm: August 8, 2011

http://www.sacred-texts.com/neu/celt/mab/mab22.htm: October 5, 2010

http://en.wikipedia.org/wiki/Cúchulainn: September 29, 2010

http://en.wikipedia.org/wiki/Morgause: September 20, 2010

http://en.wikipedia.org/wiki/Liath_Macha: September 20, 2010

http://en.wikipedia.org/wiki/Fisher_King: October 26, 2010

http://en.wikipedia.org/wiki/Cessair: February 8, 2011.

http://en.wikipedia.org/wiki/Milesians_(Irish): February 8, 2011.

http://en.wikipedia.org/wiki/Fir_Bolg: February 8, 2011.

http://www.starfirescircle.com/wicca6.txt: September 3, 2010.

Index

About the Author

Christopher Penczak is an award winning author, teacher and healing practitioner. As an advocate for the timeless perennial wisdom of the ages, he is rooted firmly in the traditions of modern Witchcraft and Earth-based religions, but draws from a wide range of spiritual traditions including shamanism, alchemy, herbalism, Theosophy and Hermetic Qabalah to forge his own magickal traditions. His many books include *Magick of Reiki, The Mystic Foundation, The Three Rays of Witchcraft,* and *The Inner Temple of Witchcraft.* He is the co-founder of the Temple of Witchcraft tradition, a non-profit religious organization to advance the spiritual traditions of Witchcraft, as well as the co-founder of Copper Cauldron Publishing, a company dedicated to producing books, recordings, and tools for magickal inspiration and evolution. He has been a faculty member of the North Eastern Institute of Whole Health and a founding member of The Gifts of Grace, an interfaith foundation dedicated to acts of community service, both based in New Hampshire. He maintains a teaching and healing practice in New England, but travels extensively lecturing. More information can be found at *www.christopherpenczak.com* and *www.templeofwitchcraft.org.*

The Temple of Witchcraft
MYSTERY SCHOOL AND SEMINARY

Witchcraft is a tradition of experience, and the best way to experience the path of the Witch is to actively train in its magickal and spiritual lessons. The Temple of Witchcraft provides a complete system of training and tradition, with four degrees found in the Mystery School for personal and magickal development and a fifth degree in the Seminary for the training of High Priestesses and High Priests interested in serving the gods, spirits, and community as ministers. Teachings are divided by degree into the Oracular, Fertility, Ecstatic, Gnostic, and Resurrection Mysteries. Training emphasizes the ability to look within, awaken your own gifts and abilities, and perform both lesser and greater magicks for your own evolution and the betterment of the world around you. The Temple of Witchcraft offers both in-person and online courses with direct teaching and mentorship. Classes use the *Temple of Witchcraft* series of books and CD Companions as primary texts, supplemented monthly with information from the Temple's Book of Shadows, MP3 recordings of lectures and meditations from our founders, social support through group discussion with classmates, and direct individual feedback from a mentor.

For more information and current schedules, please visit the Temple of Witchcraft website: *www.templeofwitchcraft.org*.

CPSIA information can be obtained at www.ICGtesting.com
Printed in the USA
BVOW050325110613

322936BV00004B/84/P